Charles Gore

The Mission of the Church

Four Lectures Delivered in June, 1892, in the Cathedral Church of St. Asaph

Charles Gore

The Mission of the Church
Four Lectures Delivered in June, 1892, in the Cathedral Church of St. Asaph

ISBN/EAN: 9783337002824

Printed in Europe, USA, Canada, Australia, Japan

Cover: Foto ©Lupo / pixelio.de

More available books at **www.hansebooks.com**

THE
MISSION OF THE CHURCH

GORE

Oxford
HORACE HART, PRINTER TO THE UNIVERSITY

THE

MISSION OF THE CHURCH

FOUR LECTURES

*DELIVERED IN JUNE, 1892, IN THE CATHEDRAL
CHURCH OF ST. ASAPH*

By CHARLES GORE, M.A.

CANON OF WESTMINSTER AND HONORARY CHAPLAIN TO THE QUEEN

SIXTH THOUSAND

LONDON
JOHN MURRAY, ALBEMARLE STREET
1899

PREFACE

THIS volume contains the substance of the lectures delivered by me in the Cathedral Church of St. Asaph, about the festival of St. Peter in this year, on the subject suggested to me, viz. the Mission of the Church. The lectures were not written, and I had, when they were delivered, no intention of publishing them; but I was led to alter my determination and have here endeavoured to reproduce them in substance, with slight alterations and additions, by the help of a report published in the *Church Times*. The 'excitement,' alluded to in the opening of the first lecture, was that occasioned by the General Election then immediately approaching, which, in Wales at least, had direct reference to the position of the Church. The general argument of the lectures will indicate what is to my mind the best method of Church defence.

Before going further I should wish to express my sense of the great good which gatherings of the Clergy, such as that in which it was my privilege to take part at St. Asaph, are calculated to do. It would be indeed a good thing if in every diocese, especially every country diocese, a benefaction similar to that which pays a lecturer at St. Asaph, only too liberally, were to open the way to a similar gathering. To get a great proportion of the clergy of a diocese together during four days for common prayer and eucharist, and a course of instruction such as leads naturally to mutual enquiry, discussion and intercourse, seems to me a measure admirably calculated to meet the evils which isolation and the prevalence of spiritual apathy tend to generate in rural dioceses. Why should not the example be widely followed?

Preface. vii

I know that these lectures will be condemned by many as too ecclesiastical. 'By making so much of the Church organization,' it will be said, 'you only alienate the Nonconformists, and promote disunion.' My answer to this would be a plain one. If we believe—what the primitive Church and the New Testament documents do, as it seems to me, come near to forcing us to believe—that our Lord founded a visible Church, and that this Church with her creed and scriptures, ministry and sacraments, is the instrument which He has given us to use, our course is clear. We must devote our energies to making the Church adequate to the divine intention—as strong in principle, as broad in compass, as loving in spirit, as our Lord intended her to be; trusting that, in proportion as her true motherhood is realized, her children will find their peace within her bosom. We cannot believe that there is any religious need which at the last resort the resources of the Church are inadequate to meet.

Meanwhile it is of great importance that we

should remember that all baptized persons, even if they belong to separatist organizations, are as individuals members of the body of Christ. Surely it would be well if we Churchmen endeavoured to take every opportunity of cultivating equal and friendly *social* relations with Nonconformists. I believe Dr. Döllinger once expressed a great hope that internal reunion among Christians in England would be largely promoted by the common education of Churchmen and Nonconformists at the universities. This common education, promoting friendliness among those who are to be clergy of the Church or ministers of different religious bodies, may do much good. But may not such friendly relations be established equally well elsewhere? Such personal acquaintance is much more likely to do good than the attendance of Churchmen at Nonconformist gatherings to depreciate their own Churchmanship. This latter course of action does not appear to minister to any other result than that of promoting disunion among ourselves.

Once more, these lectures will be said to minister to sacerdotalism. There is no doubt a widespread horror of 'sacerdotalism,' but the way to meet it is not, I think, by vague denunciation or vague glorification of an undefined principle; but by careful explanation of what the Catholic principle of the apostolic succession in the ministry means, as expounded by the best theologians and verified in the documents of the New Testament. Archdeacon Farrar, in a recent denunciation of 'sacerdotalism' in the *Contemporary Review* for July of this year, has quoted some expressions of mine in repudiation of the idea of a vicarious priesthood with apparent approval. 'It is encouraging to find that the head of the Pusey House recognizes the priesthood of the English Church as *ministerial*... and says—"It is an abuse of the sacerdotal conception, if it be supposed that the priesthood exists to celebrate sacrifices or acts of worship in the place of the body of the people or as their substitutes."' May I assure the archdeacon that I am not separating myself from other High Churchmen or from Catholic theologians as a whole, in maintaining the ministerial and representative character of the Christian priesthood?

No doubt, however, as all the best things are most liable to corruption, so there is a reality corresponding to what is denounced as ecclesiastical exclusiveness and sacerdotal pride. It is in view of this that the Rev. E. F. Russell, of St. Alban's, Holborn, after speaking of the late well-known vicar of that Church as one of those who 'to some extent at least, have realized in their own person those revived ideals of the priesthood, its supernatural character, mission, and endowment, which are filling the hearts and firing the zeal of so many of the new generation of our clergy'—adds the words, 'Ideals of any sort are dangerous visitants to vain and shallow minds. In the thin soil of a poor nature they bear ugly fruit in arrogance, or insolent pretentiousness. It is not to be denied that instances of this "bringing forth of wild grapes" are not unknown amongst

Preface. xi

us. But it is far otherwise in the case of those loftier, nobler souls, which, thank God, are also to be found in our ranks. Upon them the dignity of the sacerdotal character, the glory of a divine trust for the good of human life, weighs with the oppression of an almost unbearable responsibility. They find in it a ground, not for self-exaltation or self-assertion, but rather for the deepest self-humiliation. They are filled with concern how they may make good its requirements. A sense of shortcoming haunts them. The vision of what should be prevents all satisfaction in that which is. Hence the feature common to the saintliest among the clergy, everywhere and in all times, of a merciless self-effacement and self-sacrifice, and, by natural consequence, an especial devotion to the cross of Christ[1].'

In fact, in proportion as we believe in our priesthood, we believe that we must live and die for men; nay more, that we must represent

---

[1] *Alexander Heriot Mackonochie* (Kegan Paul, 1890), p. ix.

men, represent what is good even in the least enlightened aspirations of people about us. This ideal is not one which, honestly pursued, will minister to anything else than humility and sympathy. For to understand men we must learn to honour them, and this is only possible to humility and self-effacement.

I have enunciated principles in this book which I have endeavoured to justify at length elsewhere. Thus the ecclesiastical principle, and the principle of the apostolic succession asserted in Lecture I, I have vindicated at length in *The Church and the Ministry* (Longmans): the Anglican position as against Rome, also asserted in Lecture I, in the *Roman Catholic Claims* (Longmans, see 3rd or 4th edit.): the orthodox position as against destructive criticism, asserted in Lecture III, in the *Bampton Lectures* of 1891 (John Murray): the position of freedom within the Church in regard to many points raised by the criticism of the Old Testament, also asserted in Lecture III, in the Essay on 'The Holy Spirit and Inspiration,' in *Lux Mundi*, and in the Preface to the 10th edition (John Murray). I must express a hope that if anyone wishes to criticize opinions which I have expressed on these subjects in the following pages, he will remember that they are justified at greater length elsewhere.

C. G.

Michaelmas, 1892.

PREFACE TO SECOND EDITION

In view of a criticism that seemed just, I have somewhat modified my Note 8, on the New Testament meaning of the word 'spiritual': otherwise I have made no alterations.

C. G.

St. Alban's Day, 1893.

CONTENTS

LECTURE I.
THE MISSION OF THE CHURCH 1

LECTURE II.
UNITY WITHIN THE CHURCH OF ENGLAND . . 39

LECTURE III.
THE RELATION OF THE CHURCH TO INDEPENDENT AND
  HOSTILE OPINION 79

LECTURE IV.
THE MISSION OF THE CHURCH IN SOCIETY . . 116

APPENDED NOTES.
1. THE WITNESS TO THE DOCTRINE OF A VISIBLE CHURCH IN
    CLEMENT AND IGNATIUS 151
2. THE RECENT CHARGE OF ARCHDEACON SINCLAIR . . 152
3. THE NECESSITY OF SACRAMENTS NOT ABSOLUTE . . 156
4. IRENAEUS ON THE ELEMENTS OF THE CHRISTIAN RELIGION 157

		PAGE
5.	THE CONTENTS OF THE NEW TESTAMENT TRADITION	157
6.	THE ANGLICAN DOCTRINE OF THE SACRAMENTS	158
7.	THE ANGLICAN REQUIREMENT OF THE APOSTOLIC SUCCESSION	159
8.	THE MEANING OF THE WORD 'SPIRITUAL'	160
9.	GNOSTIC ESOTERICISM AND CHRISTIAN UNIVERSALITY	160
10.	TERTULLIAN ON THE SIMPLICITY OF CHRISTIAN SACRAMENTS	161
11.	GOETHE ON THE SACRAMENTAL SYSTEM	161
12.	THAT CHRISTIANS HAVE NO NEED TO ASK FOR THE SPIRIT	163
13.	INFANTS WHO ARE PROPER SUBJECTS OF BAPTISM	163
14.	SCIENCE CANNOT PROCEED WITHOUT ASSUMPTIONS	165
15.	EVOLUTION AND ITS RELATION TO RELIGIOUS THOUGHT	166
16.	THE RESOLUTIONS OF THE PAN-ANGLICAN CONFERENCE ON DIVORCE	167
17.	CHRIST OUR EXAMPLE AND OUR INWARD LIFE	169

LECTURE I.

THE MISSION OF THE CHURCH.

'As my Father hath sent me, even so send I you.'
St. John xx. 21.

Reverend Father in God, my brethren of the clergy and of the laity,—If it be true, as a general rule, that the fault to which the Church in agricultural districts is specially liable is the fault of apathy and indolence, yet it is, I suppose, profoundly improbable that such would be at all the danger of the Church of Christ in Wales under present circumstances. Whatever else may be the effect of the agitation of past years and of the present moment round the walls of your spiritual building, it must at least have the effect of putting you upon your mettle. It must substitute for any tendency to indolence or apathy a condition of excitement, with what is good and what is bad in excitement. Thus we hear round about us to-day the note of encouragement; and we hear the note of fear, the presage of disaster:—the note of encouragement, because of the real progress of the Church in recent years, the note of fear, because so much is still lacking, the ground still to be made up is so vast, the dangers which threaten us are so alarming. We may have been reminded of our own mingled atmosphere of grief and joy by the lesson from Ezra which we read but a few days ago describing the state of things in Jerusalem when the builders after the captivity had 'laid again the foundation of the temple of the Lord[1]'—'All the people shouted with a great shout when they praised the Lord, because the foundation of the house of the Lord was laid. But many of the priests and Levites and chief of the fathers, who were

[1] Ezra iii. 11-13.

ancient men, that had seen the first house, when the foundation of this house was laid before their eyes, wept with a loud voice; and many shouted aloud for joy: so that the people could not discern the noise of the shout of joy from the noise of the weeping of the people.'

Now, in times of excitement, if we would be spiritually-minded, we have one supreme and paramount obligation—it is that of recalling ourselves again and again, away from the cry of the religious or political platform, to first principles, those first principles in the light of which our true life must be lived. What do we mean by being Churchmen? What is the divine mission of the Church? What is the ground of our imperishable confidence? It is—'As my Father hath sent me, even so send I you.'

I.

This is, in its ultimate terms, the mission of the Church. It is the carrying out, in its full scope, of the mission of the Christ:

'As my Father hath sent me.' God has given us a revelation of Himself in His incarnate Son; and this revelation or disclosure of God in Christ is expressed in the threefold office of Christ as prophet, priest, and king.

As prophet He not merely conveys to man a particular message about God, but He discloses God under conditions of our humanity. He is very God, Son of God; and, being God, He discloses in the intelligible terms of our humanity what God is. We look to the human mind and will and character, the human justice and love, of Jesus of Nazareth, and we know that we behold nothing else than the mind and will and character, the justice and love, of very God. Moreover what is revealed is not merely the mind or purpose of God towards men; but, within certain limits, there is a real disclosure of His inner being, of those inner relations which bind altogether in the indissoluble unity of Godhead, the Father, the Son and the Holy Ghost. Christ is prophet, then, and discloses

The Mission of the Church.

God to man; but He is also priest, to unite or reconcile man to God. In this capacity He first exhibits, in supreme perfection and fulness, that unity with God of which our nature is capable. In His own person He represents the perfect attitude of man to God. In His own person He offers, in our name and on our behalf, the sacrifice of perfect homage to the divine righteousness, which our sins had been continuously outraging. All this He does first in His own person independently of us and in our stead; but what He first does for us, He proceeds to do in us. He takes us up into union with Himself. We share His manhood, His communion with God, His self-oblation to the Father. Thus He is our priest. Thirdly, He is king; because He comes forth to make His moral claim felt upon our manhood: to redeem and to liberate it, to subdue and to govern it, in all its parts and faculties. Thus He is prophet, priest, and king; and, as His Father hath sent Him on this prophetic, priestly, kingly mission, so in

His turn in the persons of His apostles He sends out His Church. 'As my Father hath sent me, even so send I you.'

The Church perpetuates the mission of her Master—prophetic, priestly, kingly.

She perpetuates the prophetic mission of Christ, because she carries down through the ages, as its pillar and ground, the truth which once for all was disclosed in Jesus, the truth involved in His person, God and man; the truth about God, which He disclosed in His life, His works, His words; the truth about man, his destiny, his capacity, and the sin which has marred his destiny, and separated him from God; and the truth about redemption, the redemption wrought out by God in Christ. This truth involved in the person of our redeemer, Jesus, it is the prophetic office of the Church perpetually to bear witness to, to place continuously before the eyes of men, to inculcate again and again in its varied adaptation to the different needs of different ages. Again, the Church goes forth to perpetuate the priestly mission of Christ. For the work of Christ is not perpetuated merely in words; there is more to be done than teaching. 'The kingdom of God is not in word but in power.' There is the gift of grace, the gift of the Spirit, and manifold gifts from the Spirit in view of man's manifold needs; and the Church is the home in which this rich treasure is dispensed, the household of God in which is distributed the bread of life, a portion to each in due season. It is by the ministration of these manifold gifts of grace that our humanity is raised again into its true relation to God, and brought back into union with Him. And the Church shares also Christ's kingly function. The pastoral office is at least as much an office of ruling as of feeding. The Church is to discipline, to guide, to strengthen, the manifold characters, wills and minds of men, till this human life of ours is brought, in all its parts and capacities, into the obedience of Christ. Thus the Church perpetuates the threefold mission of the Christ. 'As my Father hath sent me prophetic, priestly, kingly, so send I you, prophetic, priestly, kingly.'

II.

Now the point which, at this stage, I wish to emphasize is that Christ has thus enshrined in a visible body, a visible Church, those gifts of truth and grace with which He has enriched mankind.

Another method might have been adopted. It is conceivable that our Lord might have proclaimed a certain body of truth, and then left it to make its own way, to advance by its own weight among mankind. He might have scattered truth at random, like 'bread upon the waters,' over the area of human need. But in fact He did something different, He enshrined the truth deliberately in an organized society; and it is, we believe, in accordance with the mind of Christ that the Church has in fact gone out into the world as a society based upon a distinctive creed, a creed gradually enshrined in formulas and appealing to a

The Mission of the Church.   9

fixed canon of sacred scriptures, representing the original teaching of Christ's Apostles.

Once more, the gifts of grace are made part of a visible system through the ministry of sacraments. What are sacraments? They are outward, visible and also social, ceremonies intended for the conveyance of spiritual gifts. There is the gift of regeneration, the gift of the indwelling of the Holy Ghost, the gift of the bread of life, the flesh and blood of Christ. Now these are spiritual gifts, and we can conceive of their having been given through purely invisible channels; in fact, they *are* given by channels which, as I say, are not only visible, but also social. Baptism, through which is conveyed the Spirit's gift of regeneration or incorporation into Christ, is an outward ceremony, and an outward ceremony which, at the same time, is social. It is a ceremony of admission into a visible society. Confirmation, by which is bestowed the indwelling of the Holy Ghost, is an act of benediction, the laying on of the hands of the chief ruler of a society upon one of its members. The Eucharist again, in which is given and taken the body and blood of Christ, is an outward ceremony, and a ceremony which, in its material basis, involves a fraternal meal. Each of the sacraments is not only a visible but also a social institution; such as involves that men are to be admitted into, and kept in relation to, a visible society.

Once again this society is not only to be a visible reality at any particular moment. It is also to be continuous down the ages. It is in view of this need that the meaning of the apostolic succession of the ministry becomes apparent. For the Church is a catholic society, that is, a society belonging to all nations and ages. As a catholic society it lacks the bonds of the life of a city or a nation—local contiguity, common language, common customs. We cannot, then, very well conceive how its corporate continuity could have been maintained otherwise than through some succession of persons such as, bearing the apostolic commission for ministry, should be in each generation the necessary centres of the Church's life. Granted this apostolic succession, there is guaranteed in the Church as a whole, and in each local church, a perpetual stewardship of the grace and truth which came by Jesus Christ, a perpetual stewardship which, at the same time, acts as the link of continuity, binding the churches of all ages and of all nations into visible unity with the apostolic college.

Thus by her creeds and her canon of scriptures, by her sacraments and her apostolic succession, the Church is rendered necessarily a visible body. It is spiritual in its aim. It exists for no other purpose than to minister to the spiritual union of man with God. It is spiritual in its aim and essence, but it is visible in fact on earth. The invisible gift is conveyed through visible channels: the invisible essence is enshrined in a visible body.

Of this doctrine of the visible Church we may say that it is first natural and second historical. Its intimate correspondence with the principle of the Incarnation we shall have the opportunity of noticing in the next lecture.

First it is natural: it corresponds to a law

of our nature. Aristotle said long ago that man is a 'social animal.' The meaning of this is that though society is made up of individuals, and indeed the aim of society is the development of the faculties of the individual, yet man realizes his individuality only by relations to a society. It is the society that makes him man, it is the social life of the nation or the city that enables the individual to become truly human.

The moral philosophy of the last, and of the early part of the present century was characterized by individualistic theories, according to which men were regarded as primarily individuals and only secondarily as members of society. But it is noticeable that modern ethical writers, even of a non-theistic school, such as Mr. Leslie Stephen and Mr. Alexander, exhibit a return to the Aristotelian principle. 'We must take society and the individual as we find them in fact,' says Mr. Alexander, 'the latter with ties that bind him to others, the former as something which we have never known to be formed by the mere coalescence of separate

The Mission of the Church.

and independent individuals[1].' It is, then, in correspondence with a fundamental law of man's social nature that the religion of the Son of Man should not deal with us first as isolated individuals; that it should present itself as a society incorporating individuals and developing the individual life by first absorbing it. It is because man is social that 'the perfect man'[2] is to be realized, not by the single Christian, but by the whole Church.

Secondly, this theory of the Church is historical—the title-deeds of Christianity establish it. Historical proof is a long matter. It cannot be given fully in a single lecture, but I may refer to one or two chief elements in it.

1. The method of Christ. We can conceive, as I have said, easily enough how our Lord might have cast the truth which He came to teach mankind broadcast over society, and left it to make its own way. But the more you examine the gospels, the more you will note that His

---

[1] Alexander, *Moral Order and Progress* (Trübner, 1889), p. 96.
[2] Eph. iv. 13 [R.V.].

method was not in fact this, but the opposite. More and more He concentrates all His efforts upon that little band beside Him, whom by steady discipline He was preparing to be the nucleus of His new and distinctive society. On this vigil of St. Peter's Day, we naturally notice this more particularly: He turned away from our human nature as He found it, unsatisfactory and inadequate, when He wished to lay His new foundation. 'He did not commit himself to men ... for He knew what was in man.' Those faults in our human nature, which in every generation have turned philanthropists into cynics, and driven the wisest wellnigh mad—that unsatisfactoriness of our fallen manhood—Jesus knew from the first. Therefore He waited, He laboured, He prayed in our true manhood till He had prepared the soil which should be adequate for the seed He meant to sow in it; till He had found a foundation, not like the shifting sand of ordinary fallen manhood, but strong and rock-like, on which He could build; and this rock-like character our human nature was to

The Mission of the Church.

gain only through faith in Himself complete and entire. Thus, when He had gained from the lips of St. Peter an adequate confession of His name, a confession different altogether from the vague and shifting ideas about Himself which were current among the people generally, then it was that He could make a beginning with His new spiritual structure. He turned to Peter, the representative of the new confession, and said, 'Blessed art thou, Simon Bar-Jonah; for flesh and blood hath not revealed it unto thee, but my Father which is in heaven. And I also say unto thee, that thou art Peter—Rockman—and upon this rock I will build my church, and the gates of death shall not prevail against it[1].' We know the subsequent history. The faith of Peter was shared by the apostolic college, and the promise to Peter was, as the Christian fathers perceived, fulfilled to the whole apostolic company in their common commission: 'As my

[1] St. Matt. xvi. 17, 18. Cf. Holland's *Creed and Character*, Serm. III. 'The Rock of the Church' (Longmans).

Father hath sent me, even so send I you.' And the meaning of this whole history is, that Jesus did, with all deliberation, establish a distinct society to represent the kingdom of God on earth, a society distinct from humanity at large, based upon the explicit confession of His name. Consider further the method of Christ, the institution of social sacraments, baptism and the eucharist, and you will find that it becomes to your mind a more and more luminous truth, that our Lord was constituting, to last till He should 'come again,' one visible fraternity, the company of His 'elect' in which to enshrine the spiritual life which was to have its source in Himself.

2. Now let us read, from this point of view, the apostolic writings; and we shall notice with what clearness the religion of Jesus Christ appears in history as a visible society, and nothing else than a visible society. Its story is told simply enough in the Acts of the Apostles. In that book being a Christian means nothing else than membership in the visible body, the Church. The Church ad-

vances from place to place, but the local bodies, 'the churches,' are the expansions of 'the Church'[1]—based upon the 'apostles' doctrine,' continuing in the 'apostles' fellowship,' and governed by the common apostolic authority[2]. The same truth is apparent in St. Paul's epistles —not only in the Epistle to the Ephesians, or in the Pastoral Epistles in which he is specially making provision for the Church's future in view of his own death, but also in an epistle of an earlier period. Observe in the First Epistle to Corinth, where St. Paul is dealing with the lamentable case of incest in the young church there, how instinctively clear to his mind is the distinction between 'those within' and 'those without[3].' Christianity is not a set of opinions which people may hold, as in fact people in India to-day do hold, more or less, the truth about Christ over a wide area of Hindoo society. To be a Christian means to be within that apostolic society, which was made up of good and evil mingled together, as

---

[1] Acts ix. 31; xi. 26; xiii. 1; xv. 41; xvi. 5.
[2] Acts xv. 28.　　　　　　　[3] 1 Cor. v. 9-13.

this incestuous man, and those aiding and abetting him, were as tares among the wheat, in the young community at Corinth.

3. Let us pass to the sub-apostolic Church. We should all of us make ourselves familiar with those very short writings, the Epistle of Clement and the Epistles of Ignatius. The Epistle of Clement was written about the same time as St. John's Gospel, in the West, at Rome. It comes, then, from under the immediate shadow of apostolic influence and teaching; yet notice how unquestionably this doctrine of the visible Church is its characteristic mark. There is no conception of Christianity there discoverable, except this conception of an actual society, with its divinely established order and its officers commissioned by apostolic authority[1].

You turn from the West, from Clement, from the influence of St. Peter and St. Paul, to Ignatius, in the East, to the sphere of the influence of St. John, and still you find the same thing. Read the letters of Ignatius the martyr, written about A. D. 110, on his way to

[1] See appended note 1.

The Mission of the Church.

death. He is hard pressed to deliver his message to the churches before he is taken away. And the central interest of his message is twofold. It lies first in the paramount necessity which he discovers in the truth of the Incarnation, that Christ, the very Son of God, did really take our human nature; and secondly in his insistence upon the truth that God's message to man is enshrined in those visible societies which have for their ministers bishops, priests, and deacons, 'without which three orders no Church has a title to the name [1].'

4. As we move down the record of history we find the Church in different parts of the world assuming different characteristics. In the West, where the Roman genius prevails, the special characteristic is that of order and discipline. In Alexandria Christianity is regarded primarily as the truth, which is to attract, to satisfy, to educate, the intellect and life of man. But this variety in the local characteristics of churches only throws into higher relief the

[1] Ign. *ad Trall.* 3, Lightfoot's trans.

common underlying creed and conception of the visible Church. In regard to the Church, its sacraments, its ministry, there is no hesitation. The idea of a number of individuals combining to form a church of their own with an organization developed out of themselves is one which, if heard of at all, as among the Montanists, is heard of only to be repudiated. Of the common doctrine of the Church I will quote only one specimen, and it shall be from Tertullian—a passage in which he declares that, whatever doctrine may be matter of dispute, this at least cannot be. 'Christ Jesus, our Lord,' he says[1], 'so long as He was living on earth, spoke Himself either openly to the people, or apart to His disciples. From amongst these He had attached to His person twelve especially, who were destined to be the teachers of the nations. Accordingly, when one of these had fallen away, the remaining eleven received His command, as He was departing to the Father, after His resurrection, to go and teach the nations, who were to be baptized into the Father and the

[1] Tertull. *de praescr.* 20.

The Mission of the Church.

Son, and the Holy Spirit. At once, then, the Apostles, whose mission this title indicates, after adding Matthias to their number, as the twelfth, in the place of Judas, on the authority of the prophecy in David's Psalm, and after receiving the promised strength of the Holy Ghost to enable them to work miracles and preach, first of all bore witness to the faith in Judæa and established churches, and afterwards, going out into the world, proclaimed the same teaching of the same faith to the nations, and forthwith founded churches in every city, from which all other churches in their turn have received the tradition of the faith and the seeds of doctrine; yes, and are daily receiving, that they may become churches; and it is on this account that they too will be reckoned apostolic, as being the offspring of apostolic churches. Every kind of thing must be referred to its origin. Accordingly, many and great as are the churches, yet all is that one first Church which is from the Apostles, that one whence all are derived. So all are the first, and all are apostolic, while all together prove their unity; while the fellowship of peace, and the title of brotherhood, and the interchange of hospitality remain amongst them—rites which are based on no other principle than the one handing down of the same faith.'

III.

'I believe in one Holy Catholic Church.' This act of faith puts us in opposition to current 'undenominationalism,' and, as we hold it in the Anglican Church, to the *exclusive* claim of the Roman communion. Both oppositions must be briefly considered.

Undenominationalism. By this name I refer to the theory which represents men as first becoming Christians by an act of individual faith, and, after that, combining into Christian societies, greater or smaller, as suits their predilections[1]. This, you observe, is the opposite of the theory that men become Christians, in the first instance, by incorporation into the one Christian society, and then, after that, are bound to realize individually their Christian

[1] See app. note 2.

The Mission of the Church.

privileges. This second theory, if what I have been saying is true, is the one which alone is sanctioned in the original documents of Christianity. Whether it seems therefore at any particular moment advantageous or disadvantageous—in any case we are not responsible for it. It is part of that which comes to us from Jesus Christ our Master; but yet the objections to it on the undenominational side are sufficiently clear to demand that we should consider what they mean.

'This doctrine of the Church seems reasonable enough, as you state it,' people say, 'and we recognize the strength of its appeal to the New Testament and primitive Christian traditions. But if it comes seriously to believing it, one must ask, Is it not in too manifest conflict with facts? This suggestion of exclusive channels of grace, does it square with facts, with the wide and promiscuous diffusion of spiritual excellence as the record of history and the experience of life present it? Nay! I must have a freer theory. Verily "the wind bloweth where it listeth"—so is the movement of the free Spirit.'

Ah, yes! who could deny it? The Spirit breatheth where He listeth. All life is His in nature and in man. There is no being which lies outside the action of the eternal Word or His Spirit. Every movement of good in man anywhere is of His breathing. Everywhere, under His inspiration, men are seeking after God, 'if haply they may feel after Him and find Him,' and 'in every nation he that feareth God and worketh righteousness,' feareth and worketh with the help of the Holy Spirit, and in Him is accepted of God. Thus, though in Hooker's words[1], 'It is not *ordinarily* God's will to bestow the grace of sacraments on any, but by the sacraments'; yet God is not tied to any special channels. There are no such things as exclusive means of grace, means of grace as to which one can say, 'God worketh here, not elsewhere.' But this, after all, is no novel concession. 'Deus non alligatur sacramentis suis,' it was said of old. 'His ordinances are laws for us, not for Him[2].' In all ages thoughtful theologians of almost all schools

[1] *E. P.* v. 57. 4.   [2] See app. note 3.

have seen that this truth is involved in the recognition of the fatherhood of God, and His all-rectifying and impartial justice. But then, the rejoinder comes, what is it you claim for the sacraments? Just what is involved in the idea of 'covenant,' and in the idea of 'the household' of God. The state of covenant carries us into a region beyond that of dim and anxious seeking. It involves a clear disclosure of Himself by God, and, corresponding with this, clear and distinct bestowals and promises of grace. A household is a place where food and nurture is definitely and systematically provided. The joy of Christians is the joy of sons in their father's household, children of the covenant. This is what we claim for sacraments: not that they are exclusive channels of grace, so that God cannot give except through them the gifts of His love; but that through them only, as elements in His unique covenant, are definite graces pledged and guaranteed by the Divine fidelity; so that the faithful Christian transcends the conditions of anxious enquiry and passes into the region where he faithfully welcomes the assured gift, and fearlessly uses it as indeed given.

And if you press the question further, and ask, 'Does not your theory of the security of the covenant involve the conception of "valid sacraments"—sacraments, that is, that are only valid when they are celebrated by persons properly ordained in the due transmission of apostolical authority? and does not this theory leave out of account what is, at least in Anglo-Saxon Christianity, an immense and solid part of the working force of Christianity?'—I answer, We must hold to this doctrine of apostolic succession as bound up with the validity of some at least of the sacraments. The idea of an ordained stewardship of divine gifts is inseparably associated both in idea and in history with the sacramental system. But what is meant by valid sacraments? The Greek word βέβαιος, and the Latin word 'validus,' have a definite meaning. The opposite of secure or valid is not non-existent but precarious. The fact that God promises to give in one way does not destroy His power to give in another. It were blasphemy, then, to

The Mission of the Church.

deny the Spirit's action where we see the Spirit's fruits. It is impossible for one who thinks seriously to ignore or underrate the vast debt which English Christianity owes to nonconformist bodies, to bodies which have fallen quite outside the action of the apostolic ministry. But was there not a cause? If we consider the sins, the scandalous neglect and sluggishness of the Church, is it so very wonderful that God should have worked largely and freely outside the appointed and authorized ministries? We should think it blasphemy, then, to deny the spiritual experience of the past or of the present as to the freedom of the divine action, even when the spiritual experience is only viewed from outside. Still less could we dream of asking anyone who is not himself a Churchman to be false to his own experience. But we may ask men to be completely true to the whole of experience.

Now one part of experience is surely the disastrous present effect of our divisions. No serious Christian can fail to desire most earnestly restored fellowship among Christians. Something is so very wrong at present that we must ask over again, and more and more as circumstances throw back each man upon first principles, What is the divinely intended basis or form of the Christian religion? And the answer is 'by one Spirit were we all baptized into one body.' The one body—you view it in history, you trace it back to apostolic days—certainly its main lineaments are throughout unmistakeable. There have been many partial developments and causes of division, and local beliefs and changing customs and laws. But there is the one tradition of the faith in its central features constant and original: there are the apostolic scriptures, the canon of which gradually takes the place of the living authority of apostolic teachers, as the ultimate court of Christian appeal: there is the system of the sacraments: there is the apostolically commissioned ministry, with its stewardship of the gifts of truth and grace[1]. These, as parts of the organism of the Spirit, constitute for the whole of the first fifteen centuries the fabric of Christianity. Since the Reformation it is not too much to say that

[1] See app. note 4.

The Mission of the Church. 29

historical enquiry in general, and in our own days, biblical criticism, have rendered it increasingly difficult to tear the Bible out of the structure of the Church, out of the organism of which it forms a part. Nor is it possible to find in original Christianity a 'liberty of prophesying' which left men independent of the visible Church: not in apostolic days, if the Acts of the Apostles and the Pastoral Epistles and the Epistle to the Corinthians are true witnesses: not in later days, unless we do violence to the existing evidence and make of Montanism the truly conservative movement[1].

In regard to the doctrine of apostolic succession, I must say one other word. It has been, in history, too much identified with the threefold form of the ministry[2]. I believe myself that the evidence, as we have it at present, points cogently to this conclusion: that since apostolic days there have been always three orders of the ministry; not only

[1] See *The Church and the Ministry*, pp. 207-213, and app. notes H and I.
[2] See further, *The Chucrh and the Ministry*, pp. 72 ff.

deacons and presbyters (or bishops according to the earliest use of the term), but also ministers of the apostolic order, superior to the presbyters, such as Timothy and Titus, or those 'prophets' of whom we hear in the earliest Christian literature. I believe that what occurred was the gradual localization in particular churches of this apostolic order of ministers which previously had not usually been so localized, and that there was no time when presbyters or presbyter bishops had either the supreme authority of government or the power to ordain; the change which took place consisting only in the localization of an order of men previously exercising a more general supervision, and the reservation of the name 'bishop' to these localized apostolic officers.

But there are certain facts which have led some good authorities to suppose that, at one time, all the presbyters in some churches held together the chief authority in government and the power to ordain, the 'episcopate' being as it were 'in commission' among them. Now this theory has, I think, from the point

The Mission of the Church. 31

of view of ecclesiastical *principle*, been too much discussed. It does not affect the principle of apostolic succession in the least. The principle is that no man in the Church can validly exercise any ministry, except such as he has received from a source running back ultimately to the apostles, so that any ministry which a person takes upon himself to exercise, which is not covered by an apostolically received commission, is invalid.

Now, if the order of presbyters at any time held the right to ordain, that was because it had been entrusted to them by apostolic men. It no more disturbs the principle of apostolic succession than if your lordship ordained all the presbyters in this diocese to-day to episcopal functions. There would ensue a great deal of inconvenience and confusion, but nothing that would violate the principle of apostolical succession. On the other hand, the departure from this principle is manifest when presbyters in the sixteenth or subsequent century took upon themselves to ordain other presbyters. They were taking on themselves an office which, beyond all question, they had not received—which was not imparted to them in their ordination. There had been a perfectly clear understanding for many centuries what did and what did not belong to the presbyter's office. This is the principle which it is essential to maintain, and its title-deeds lie in the continuous record of Church history.

IV.

We stand, then, repudiating the undenominational conception of Christianity. On the other hand, we Anglican Churchmen stand repudiating the claim of Rome. When you state the doctrine of the visible Church, sacraments and ministry, people sometimes tell you that the Roman Church is the only logical expression of that theory. Now, historically, the Roman Church is not the development of the whole of the Church, but only of a part of it; and this historical fact would not matter so much if spiritually the Roman Church represented the whole of Christianity—

The Mission of the Church.

the whole of Christianity as it finds expression in the first Christian age, or in the New Testament. But the more accurately any one studies the subject, the more clearly he must, I think, come to see that the Roman Church, whatever be its graces, powers, and excellences, is a one-sided development of Christianity: a development of certain qualities in Christianity with which the Latin genius had special affinity, its disciplinary and governmental powers, but a development which ignored other qualities at least as certainly belonging to Christianity, such as the strengthening of individuality which it is intended to promote, the responsibility which it inculcates for personal enquiry, the love of the bare truth, the considerateness, the fairness which it ought to foster. The Roman Church does not represent the whole of Christianity, nor the whole spirit of Scripture or of the early Church. To some of us this will seem understating the truth; but a statement of the truth as far as it goes it certainly is.

Now it is not only the case that the Roman Church does not in fact represent the whole of the Christian spirit, but it is compelled by its principles to exorcize part of it, and cast it out as evil. It has committed itself to unhistorical doctrines, e.g. that the pope not only is, but has always been, infallible, that Mary was immaculately conceived, and *that these doctrines have always been recognized elements in the Catholic faith.* These dogmatic positions it puts outside the region of free enquiry and criticism. Thus it is compelled by these unhistorical dogmas to condemn the free appeal to history on matter defined by the Church, and to repudiate the responsibility of a private, i.e. personal, judgment on matters of faith. And this repudiation is bound up with a deficient appreciation of the claim of truth, intellectually and morally, for its own sake no less than for its results.

For some minds Rome is, so to speak, put out of court by positive abuses, e.g. the withdrawal of the chalice from the laity, exaggerated devotion to St. Mary and other saints, obligatory confession to the priest, compulsory celibacy of the clergy. To other minds it appears

The Mission of the Church.

a more convincing consideration that Rome is not, and cannot be, the whole of Christianity. For it is certainly true that Christianity was not meant to be narrowed as it came down the ages, or to become less and less applicable for the freeing of the whole of our manhood.

And I want to make it plain to you that this narrowing of Christianity by a development which however powerful is one-sided, coincides with the abandonment of the ancient rule of faith. The ancient rule of faith involved an appeal to Scripture as the ultimate criterion in matters of doctrine and morals. Nothing could be required of a Christian as an article of faith which could not be proved out of Scripture. This great principle secured the Church from the danger of an accumulation of dogmas such as the Roman development has in fact brought with it. The doctrine of the Immaculate Conception, the doctrine of the Treasury of Merits, with its correlative in Indulgences, have the effect of narrowing the appeal of Christianity by excluding large classes of minds who desire historical evidence for historical facts, and who resent the undue accumulation of spiritual power in the hands of ecclesiastical authorities. But these doctrines could not have been propounded as articles of faith so long as the appeal to Scripture was legitimately retained. There is nothing in Scripture which can even with specious pretence be appealed to on their behalf. Thus it is that the maintenance of the ancient appeal to Scripture is the main security that the faith shall not be narrowed as the centuries go on. It shall develop but not narrow. It is by this appeal to Scripture that Anglicanism stands or falls in its controversy with Rome. Yes, and it is able to make it stand.

We have no cause to apologize for our position; we have cause rather to be thankful for it. Anglicanism represents a combination which, if Christianity is to do its work, must exist and be amongst the most beneficent forces of catholicity in the world. It is the glory of the Anglican Church that at the Reformation she repudiated neither the ancient structure of Catholicism, nor the new and freer movement. Upon the ancient structure—the creeds, the

The Mission of the Church. 37

canon, the hierarchy, the sacraments—she retained her hold while she opened her arms to the new learning, the new appeal to Scripture, the freedom of historical criticism and the duty of private judgment. No doubt she made mistakes. But in the main she approved herself a wise steward, bringing forth out of her treasury things new and old. Therefore it is that she stands in such a unique condition of promise at the present moment among the Churches of Christendom.

I believe then in one Holy Catholic Church. This visible structure of the Church is imperfect as you see it at present; imperfect in its unity, because human arrogance and impatience have brought about division; imperfect in catholicity, because human slackness has left so large a part of the world still outside its area; imperfect in sanctity through the lawlessness of human sin. Still it is this structure which has been given to us, in and through which to work for God. In its authorization and in its possibilities it remains divine.

Can I express the reality of our responsibility for the Church, or the limits to our responsibility, better than in words we read yesterday? 'Mordecai said to Esther, If thou altogether holdest thy peace at this time, then shall there enlargement and deliverance arise to the Jews from another place; but thou and thy father's house shall be destroyed; and who knoweth whether thou art not come to the kingdom for such a time as this [1]?' That is, first: We cannot destroy the Church of God. As that lies outside our responsibilities in its structure, so it lies outside our power to destroy it. The gates of death shall not prevail against it; and no failure or sin on our part can imperil it. However we behave 'Enlargement and deliverance shall arise to the Jews—to the Israel of God—from another place.' But in our own particular district of responsibility, or within ourselves, we can destroy the Church of God. 'Thou and thy Father's house shall be destroyed.' And if there is trial here, is there not opportunity also? 'Who knoweth whether thou art not come to the kingdom for such a time as this?'

[1] Esther iv. 14.

LECTURE II.

UNITY WITHIN THE CHURCH OF ENGLAND.

'But the wisdom that is from above is first pure, then peaceable, gentle, and easy to be entreated, full of mercy and good fruits, without partiality and without hypocrisy.'
St. James iii. 17.

Reverend Father in God, my brethren of the clergy and of the laity,—The Church, we saw, is a visible society; that is, an organized body with distinctive rites, officers, conditions of membership. But the elements in her constitution which render her a visible society do not disqualify her for permanence or catholicity. Her definite creed, her fixed canon of sacred books, her sacraments, her ministry, belong to no particular epoch and no particular race or kind of men; they belong to what is simply human in us; they are as well fitted for one age as for another: that is to say, they are elements in an institution intended for universality—the Catholic Church. They belong to us therefore to-day, in our special opportunities and difficulties, as truly as they belonged to any section of the Church in past time. Now, if with this conviction we look around and ask ourselves whether the Church here and now is making full use of the materials with which God's bounty has supplied it for the conversion and edification of mankind, or if not, why not, we are struck at once with what is obviously the main present hindrance to our effectiveness—I mean our divisions.

The acuteness of the divisions inside our own Church is less, I suppose we may say with thankfulness, than it was some years ago. Parties in the Church have been brought more together. It has been the main advantage, perhaps, of Church meetings, whether diocesan or general—Diocesan Conferences or Church Congresses—that they have brought men of different schools to know, under-

Unity within the Church of England. 41

stand and tolerate one another better; and there is undoubtedly, speaking generally, less strain in England among religious parties than there was. They are merging more the one into the other. They are learning more the one from the other. The great streams of Church revival are undoubtedly fusing in their result, their issue, their influence. In a word, we are less divided than we were; but still far more divided than we ought to be. Internal divisions still constitute an immense hindrance. We are to consider them this afternoon.

I.

The Church of England provides us with a definite limit to division—or at least to legitimate division—in providing us with a rule of faith. What is this Anglican rule of faith in principle, and to what does it appeal? I cannot answer this question better than by recalling to your minds the fact that the Convocation which imposed on the clergy subscription to the Articles of Religion, issued a canon to preachers enjoining them to 'teach nothing in their sermons which they should require to be devoutly held and believed by the people except what is agreeable to the doctrine of the Old and New Testaments and what the ancient fathers and catholic bishops have collected out of the said doctrine.' The English Church appeals in some sense to Holy Scripture and Catholic tradition.

If we examine the earliest document of Christianity we find that the Apostles taught a certain body of truth which was to be the mould of Christian character. This was called from the first 'the tradition,' 'the apostles' doctrine,' 'the faith once for all delivered to the saints[1].' St. Paul recognizes in this tradition a limit even to his own teaching: 'Though we, or an angel from heaven, preach any other gospel unto you than that which we have preached unto you, let him be accursed[2].' This tradition, then, was the thing handed over once for all to the Church. The Church

[1] 2 Thess. iii. 6; Gal. i. 9; Acts ii. 42; Jude 3. Cf. Rom. vi. 17.
[2] Gal. i. 8.

was to be 'the pillar and ground of the truth [1],' because, as a visible society, she was entrusted with the task of handing on this tradition of faith and life [2].

If we now pass beyond the apostolic period we find this tradition of the faith—which later down was embodied in the Creed—being taught in the sub-apostolic churches; so that when the Christians of this period were confronted with the Gnostic heresy, they met the loose and shifting forms of idealism which are grouped under this name by an appeal to the consent of the apostolic churches. 'Look,' they said, 'at the various churches, and you find them teaching the same creed. They cannot have got to such agreement by accident.' So Tertullian put it in his incomparable epigram: 'Is it possible that so many churches of such importance should have hit, by an accident of error, on an identical creed [3]?'

---

[1] 1 Tim. iii. 15.   [2] See app. note 5.
[3] *De praescr.* 28: 'Ecquid verisimile ut tot ac tantae (ecclesiae) in unam fidem erraverint.'

This tradition constitutes the primary teaching for Christians. Look at the New Testament: you find it is not intended for primary teaching. Every book of the New Testament is manifestly written for the edification of people who had been already instructed in the doctrine of the Church. Thus if you look at the preface to St. Luke's Gospel, you find that St. Luke's object in writing is that Theophilus may know more accurately and more fully what he had already become familiar with by oral instruction. So St. Paul, St. Peter, St. James, St. Jude, St. John, and the author of the Epistle to the Hebrews imply that they write to remind or recall or edify those who had been already instructed in the rudiments of faith and life[1]. The Church, then, is the primary teacher; the Church tradition is to constitute the first lesson.

What, then, is the function of Holy Scripture? It is to be the perpetual criterion of teaching. It is the quality of tradition that it deteriorates, it becomes one-sided. Thus

---

[1] See 1 Cor. xi. 23; xv. 1-3; Gal. i. 8-9; Heb. v. 12; 2 Peter i. 12; James 1-19 [R. V.]; Jude 3; 1 John ii. 20.

there is no doubt that Christian doctrine would have undergone considerable alteration if there had been no court of appeal. The departure from primitive doctrine which in fact took place in the mediaeval Church was, as I have said, mainly due to the fact that the Church abandoned this constant appeal to Holy Scripture as that which is the sole final criterion of the faith. The Church, then, is the primary teacher; the Bible is the final court of appeal in all matters which concern the faith and morals of the Christian Church. 'The Church to teach, the Bible to prove'— that is the rule of faith.

II.

On the basis of this rule of faith, let us now consider what in fact is the doctrine which the Church of England sets before us as authoritative.

1. She sets before us, first of all, the Creeds. The Creeds give us the doctrine of God; God as He is revealed in Christ; God in His triune being, Father, Son, and Holy Ghost. Also the

doctrine of the incarnation of the Son of God, who being God, for our sakes was made man. Also the doctrine of the ministry of the Holy Spirit in the Church—one, holy, catholic and apostolic. Also, finally, the doctrine of the resurrection of the body and of eternal judgment.

Now all these are parts of the universal and primitive tradition of the Church, and they respond to the requirement of the appeal to Scripture. We do not get them from the Bible in the sense that each one picks his religion for himself out of the book; but, taught by the Church, we find them in the Bible.

2. Passing now beyond what is given us in creeds, we come to the Catechism. The Catechism lays down what is to be known and believed by every Christian at starting. Therefore it incorporates and interprets the creed. It gives us also a moral rule of life in the Ten Commandments, with their interpretation. Then a rule of worship and sacramental life. The Lord's Prayer is rightly treated not as one prayer among many, but as a pattern and type

Unity within the Church of England. 47

of all Christian prayer. And the sacraments are interpreted for us in the instances of Baptism and the Eucharist, as ordained modes of communion with Christ. All these elements in the Catechism have formed part of the tradition of the Church from the first; and again they are justified by reference to the New Testament. The same may be said of the doctrine implied in the services with which all are intended to be acquainted—the services of Baptism, Confirmation, Matrimony, Ordination—which more or less supplement, on the sacramental side, the teaching of the Catechism.

3. Beyond this, we have the Articles. Of the Articles you find a certain number, and those the most definite, are occupied with restating the truths of the Creed[1]. Four others[2] are occupied with laying down the principles of the rule of faith—the authority of the Church in matters of doctrine, the truth of the Creeds, and the necessity of the appeal to Scripture. Whilst the inspiration of Holy Scripture is implied, there is no special doctrine laid down

[1] Artt. I-V.   [2] Artt. VI-VIII and XX.

in regard to its particular nature or limits. In other Articles[1] we have clear statements as to original sin, on the principle of justification by faith, and on other matters of less importance. If you look further you will find, the more carefully you study them, that in many respects their language is studiedly vague. It is the purpose of a dogma to define. For example, when the Arian controversy arose, and the Greek Creed was re-moulded to repudiate the teaching which undermined the Godhead of our Lord, the effort was to seize the exact point of the controversy, and, by the selection of the most definite term possible, to exclude and condemn what was regarded as subversive of the whole basis of Christian doctrine and life.

On some central points the Church of England possesses, as has just been pointed out, definite and explicit dogmas; but in regard to many matters which were in controversy at the period of the Reformation, on points which belonged respectively to the Calvinistic, Lutheran, and Tridentine positions, you find

[1] Artt. IX–XI.

that, as a matter of fact, the Articles appear to have been intended not as definite solutions but rather as 'articles of peace'; they aim at shelving rather than defining questions. You have quite definitely Calvinistic articles formulated at the period of the Reformation and Lutheran articles and Tridentine decrees: but the Articles of the Church of England on points then in controversy lack the definiteness of the Lutheran, or Calvinistic, or Tridentine decisions. And we may be thankful the Church of England did not commit herself. Indefinite *formulæ* are not indeed satisfactory. They may appear to say much and in fact say little. This is, I think, the case with many of our articles. But none of greater definiteness drawn up at that moment could have failed to commit us to what, in the great issue, would have imperilled our position. The moment was one of transition and movement. It is very untrue to call it a moment of settlement. This is apparent in retrospect. What has become of definite Calvinism and definite Lutheranism all over Europe? Has Rome stopped at the Tridentine position? Had the sixteenth century the materials at its disposal which are necessary for understanding the early history of Christian doctrine? However unsatisfactory then the articles are positively as statements of truth, they are satisfactory in what they are not. It is the very fact that the Church of England at the Reformation did not commit herself to any one of the three then dominant tendencies, which leaves us now at the present moment in a unique position of hopefulness among the Churches of Europe. We are left standing firm on the Creeds, the Sacraments, the apostolic succession of the ministry; and on that basis we are to rise with the help of the clearer knowledge we now have, to the full apprehension and presentation of the ancient faith.

Thus for example in the case of the Sacraments, if we seek to know what the Church of England lays down for our acceptance, you find certain broad limits of belief clearly marked, and within these a space which is left without further definition. On the one hand, the Church of England in the latter part of the Catechism, in the offices of Baptism and Holy Communion and in the 25th Article, excludes the Zwinglian view, according to which the sacraments are merely symbols. In repudiation of this view the article accepts the mediæval definition of sacraments as 'effectual signs of grace' (*efficacia signa gratiae*), i. e. symbolic acts which not only symbolize but also effect or convey what they symbolize—God Himself, according to His promise, working invisibly on the occasion of each visible ceremony[1]. On the other hand, the Church of England repudiates certain current mediæval doctrines in regard to the sacraments ; as, for instance, the mediæval doctrine of Transubstantiation, which is declared, among other things, by denying the reality of the outward part of the sacrament of the Eucharist, to overthrow the nature of a sacrament, which has an outward and natural as well as an inward and supernatural part.

Once again, in regard to Holy Order, the Church of England requires the maintenance of the apostolic succession. She confines her

[1] See app. note 6.

ministry to those who have been actually ordained in this manner. She does not require the re-ordination of Roman Catholic priests who join the Anglican communion, but she does require ministers of religious bodies who have not received episcopal ordination to be ordained afresh. Thus she requires that men should in fact have received their ministry by apostolic succession, whereas on the other hand she does not require any exact or explicit expression of belief in regard to it [1]. Once more, in regard to Confirmation, the language of the service implies the bestowal of the Holy Spirit on the occasion—the gift of the Spirit and the Spirit's gifts—but there is no exact expression of belief required in regard to the nature of the bestowal.

Obviously, whether we like it or not, we are left with certain clear limits of belief laid down, and within these limits a considerable space is left open within which different opinions are permissible and possible.

For my own part, it seems to me a very toler-

[1] See app. note 7.

able state of things that a Church should subsist on a very limited amount of positive dogmatic requirement, on the basis of which the individual teacher and the individual learner shall grow together into a fuller perception of the whole meaning of the Catholic faith.

III.

On the basis of dogmatic requirement which I have thus endeavoured to state let us consider what is the position of the most conspicuous parties in the Church of England. I mean those three traditional parties of which we have been accustomed to speak as High, Low, and Broad. Speaking generally, their genesis and characteristics are sufficiently apparent. The High Church party has been traditionally identified with the assertion and maintenance of what we should call ecclesiastical, sacerdotal and sacramental principle. The Evangelical party has been specially associated, on the other hand, with the maintenance of principles such as circle round the doctrine of justification by faith, and the necessity of conversion. The less-defined Broad Church party has had for its most characteristic positive function—by distinction from what it has disparaged or denied—to emphasize good moral living as the one end and test of Christianity : to maintain the principle that all truth which is preached, all ordinances ministered, are to be judged by the tendency to promote good Christian living.

Obviously each of these three positions is rooted in something which the Church of England undoubtedly maintains. What is presumably the case is that the maintenance of truth in each case has become by reaction more or less one-sided, and there has been consequently antagonism through want of correlation. This suggestion it will be worth our while to consider in some detail.

I will start from the point of view of sacramentalism—the point of view of the High Churchman. He maintains the principle that the system of the Church, with her apostolic ministry and sacraments, is the divinely appointed framework of the spiritual religion. This principle I will endeavour to interpret,

Unity within the Church of England. 55

and show its relation to the points of view identified respectively with Evangelicalism and Broad Churchmanship.

The 'spiritual' religion. What is meant by this term? In religious discussions among us the term is always being used and yet not very often defined. In the ordinary English mind the term 'spiritual' still carries with it associations of indefiniteness. The 'spiritual' is supposed to be opposed to the 'material,' and so to anything tangible, visible, definite; or 'spiritual' is opposed to what is 'literal' in interpretation—it is metaphorical, and so again indefinite.

Thus external ordinances, because they are external, rules that are definite, because they are definite, truths that are exactly stated, because they are exactly stated, are more or less commonly supposed to be unspiritual and contrary to the character of the spiritual religion.

Now this state of mind is in fact due to a fundamental mistake which a little steady thinking ought to uproot.

To consider the question as a matter of

language. 'Spiritual' in the New Testament is not generally opposed to what is material or visible, but rather to what is carnal—to that in which the higher part of our nature is dragged at the heels of the lower[1]. Thus the birth of Isaac is spiritual—'he was born,' St. Paul says, 'after the spirit'; while the birth of Ishmael is carnal 'after the flesh[2],' not because the birth of Isaac was one whit less visible or material than the birth of Ishmael, but because it came about so as to express a spiritual and divine purpose, and not as the outcome of mere physical passion. Or, again, what is spiritual may be opposed to what is formal—to an act, that is, which is external only and has no moral meaning behind it. So St. Paul speaks of circumcision which is 'in the letter,' that is, in external form only, and not 'in the spirit,' as having nothing moral corresponding to it[3]; but, on the other hand, the supremely spiritual act, the act of Christ when 'in His eternal spirit He offered Himself without spot to God,' gains its meaning

---

[1] See app. note 8.   [2] Gal. iv. 29; cf. 1 Cor. x. 3, 4.
[3] Rom. ii. 29.

through its being visible and enacted in the flesh—it was an 'offering of the body of Jesus Christ once for all[1].' There is indeed one passage where 'spiritually' seems to mean metaphorically or allegorically in the matter of interpretation, the passage in the Apocalypse in which the city is spoken of, 'which spiritually is called Sodom and Egypt[2],' where it is implied that these sinful places have a mystical meaning, because their sinfulness represented a principle wider than themselves. But this use of the word 'spiritually' is unique in the New Testament, and in itself it only implies that certain definite outward objects and incidents enshrine eternal principles.

Positively, then, what does the New Testament language teach us to understand by the spiritual religion, as opposed to what is carnal or formal or unreal? The central idea of the spirit is that of life: the Christian Church is spiritual because in a unique sense she, on her pentecostal birthday, received the communication of divine life, in its threefold form of

[1] Heb. ix. 14; x. 10.   [2] Rev. xi. 8.

power, of knowledge and of love. The spirit is power: as for the 'letter'—the written laws of the Old Covenant—it could effect nothing. It could inform the conscience or terrify it, but it could not strengthen the will and make it effective for good; but the Spirit gave life, so that the 'requirement of the law' is 'fulfilled in us who walk after the Spirit[1].' Again, the Spirit is knowledge: as for the ritual ordinances of the old law they were dumb forms; they carried with them little information, or such information as witnessed to their own inadequacy; but the Spirit fulfils the heart of the Christian with a joyful intelligence of the mind and character of God, a happy insight into the meaning of all he is required to do. Once more, the Spirit is love: as for the old law, it laid injunctions upon men, which had to be obeyed, simply as they were enjoined, with nothing more than the obedience of slaves; but the men of the New Covenant have received the Spirit of God, and, one spirit with Him, they act in conscious correspondence with His

[1] Rom. viii. 4.

redemptive purpose, and serve in the glad cooperation of loving sons.

Power; intelligence; love; power from God, intelligence of God and His purposes, love to God in Himself and in His creatures—these make up the content of spirituality. But power, intelligence, love, as they are represented in human beings, beings of body and of soul, beings linked to one another in outward fellowship, can be in no sort of opposition to the world of matter and form. So holy is this human flesh, this thing of matter and form, that the Son of God has taken it for ever into His own person, and glorified it in the Godhead. Acts the most spiritual, then, like the sacrifice of Jesus, are not one whit less spiritual because they are external; truth, the more spiritually it is known, is so known as to be expressed the more exactly; life, the more spiritual it is, becomes the more definite in purpose and concrete in result. The acceptable worship, the worship 'in spirit and in truth[1],' is as much an external worship as that supreme worship which the Son of Man offered

---
[1] St. John iv. 24.

to the Father in the sacrifice of Calvary, or offers still at the glory of the right hand; but it is worship which enlists all the full energy of will, and intelligence, and love.

The Christian Church had very early in her career an opportunity of showing that she did not conceive spirituality to be in any antagonism at all to external religion. She came out in her earliest history into a philosophical atmosphere impregnated with what is called 'dualism'— that is, the assertion of the antagonism of the flesh and the spirit. Greek philosophy in its youth, in spite of its intense realization of the beauty of outward form, never succeeded in shaking off this delusion: upon its old age it returned with powerful reinforcements and brought it into captivity. The reinforcements lay in that wave of Oriental influence which in the early centuries of our era flooded our Western world. All the then prevalent sects of Gnosticism, and Manichæism, all the forms of philosophical dualism, had this in common— they thought of evil as lying, more or less completely, in the material world, in the flesh;

they thought of the material world as too low, too vile, to be in direct contact with God or the direct work of His hand; they thought that true religion lay not in the consecration of material and common things, but in getting aloof from them and separate from them. To get away from the body was to get near to God, and the highest religious state was that rapt ecstasy in which the soul, having become unconscious of all external surroundings and independent of all bodily affinities, could contemplate God. The Church's primary and great conflict was with this temper of mind as represented in Gnosticism. There is, I believe, no later struggle in which her true principles emerge so clearly, as certainly there was none in which she had to struggle so hard for very life. The opposing principles came to the front in a fourfold theory:—

(1) that the material world could not be directly the handiwork of the good God, the Father of Jesus Christ.

(2) that God could not exactly by incarnation have taken into Himself the human flesh and been born and suffered and died.

(3) that the Old Testament, as earthy and sense-bound, could not be the work of the same God as the New.

(4) that the acceptance in faith of a definite creed and definite ordinances and definite scriptures might be good enough for the vulgar and ordinary Christian, but the inner circle of the perfect and the illuminated, the spiritual men, soared above those restrictions and were independent of them.

To these positions the Christian Church in its different parts returned a blank negative.

(1) The whole world, they said, material and spiritual, is of one creation : it is rebel wills that are the source of moral evil, not material nature, which is God's work, and rightly used is very good.

(2) So good is material nature, that God has really entered into it and assumed for ever the human flesh.

(3) The Old Testament is of one piece with the New, and is to be interpreted on that principle of gradual development which is a conspicuous law of the divine working, and by

Unity within the Church of England. 63

which the spiritual destiny of the universe gradually appears.

(4) The outward ordinances, the fixed tradition and Scriptures, the ministry, sacraments, and discipline of the Church, are part of her essence and belong to her glory. They are her glory. You in the pagan world, or you who borrow the pagan principle, may have one sort of religion for the intellectual and another for the simple. But it is the glory of our religion that she puts them on the same basis; declares every man susceptible of spiritual perfection, and holds them altogether from birth to death—high and low, rich and poor, one with another[1].

Life in God, knowledge of God, communion with God, may be to the pagan only the ultimate goal of the rapt ecstatic, or the privilege of a philosophic self-abstraction from the things of sense possible to a very few: we say to all men, Take it as the gift of God, made tangible and visible in common ordinances; the submitting to be taught a creed, the reception of a washing of water and a laying on of hands;

[1] See app. note 9.

the common partaking of bread and wine, these are simple unostentatious acts, which all are capable of, which all can approach. But through these common things of the common world our God, who took, and wears, our common flesh, still communicates His hidden essence.

This was the boast of the Church; and these sacramental principles, we are bound to note, antedated long the development of ritual. Elaborate ritual is to the Catholic Churchman, who knows his principles, never more than a matter of variable expediency. At least, in early days a Christian like Tertullian was not less sacramental for being somewhat puritanical. People are scandalized, he says, by the simplicity of our sacraments: they contrast the commonness of the means with the greatness of the gift promised. The heathen rites, on the other hand, gain imposingness by pomp. But with us a man descends into the water, and a few words are spoken, and he is washed, and there is no apparatus or elaboration; and for this very reason it seems improbable that the gift of eternal life should have been conveyed.

But what a miserable incredulity, cries Tertullian, have we here, which denies to God His proper attributes — simplicity and power [1]!

The Church then is the home of the spiritual religion because she, in special and pre-eminent sense, is endowed with the Spirit of Christ, the Spirit of power and intelligence and love. And the manifold gifts of this Spirit are distributed in such a way as befits the 'household of God,' in which men are to be 'fed with their portion of meat in due season.' Each stage of life has its special need: each special need has its appropriate gift; and the appropriate gift has its ordained channel: all is ordered and simple as befits a household of security and peace. The beginning of the new life, which Christianity perpetuates from Christ, lies in that regenerating act of God upon the soul, in which by the Holy Spirit's action it is united to Christ and admitted into the fellowship of His holy body; and this regenerating act is ministered through an outward channel which is symbolical and also more, the ordinance of

[1] See app. note 10.

washing, which symbolizes and also conveys the cleansing gift of the new life. And next to birth comes strengthening. The strength of the Christian, as also his consecration to share in the priesthood and royalty of Christ, lies in the inward presence of the Holy Ghost, and this gift of the Holy Ghost is communicated since apostolic days by the laying on of hands. And the life imparted must be nourished: and again the perpetual nourishing of the new life out of the fulness of the Christ is effected through the operation of the Holy Ghost upon the simple symbolical elements of bread and wine, mingling the heavenly with the earthly things.

It is by the same principle that the general human instinct which is recognized in Christian marriage has its benediction in a special ordinance giving definiteness and sanctity to the mutual engagements of man and wife. So also that original distinction in the Christian society of the pastor and the flock is emphasized by a special ordination which solemnly conveys in outward form the consecrating and empower-

Unity within the Church of England. 67

ing of the man to his share in the apostolic ministry; and through the outward form is pledged the accompaniment of the inward qualifying gift. Once more, the scandalous sin which outrages the Christian community, or the secret sin which burdens the troubled and perplexed conscience, has its appropriate remedy in the special discipline of penitence, which, first public and then private, at one time voluntary, at another compulsory, at one time occasional, at another normal, has ever remained a permanent fact of the Church tradition—an outward ceremony of penitence and restoration, which is accompanied by a spiritual and heavenly acquittal, and is a part of that rich storage of graces with which the Church encompasses our varying needs, and leads us on from the font where she has baptized us to the death-bed where she still with holy rites ushers us into the unseen world. The Church is the home of the Spirit, whose manifold gifts are ordered and distributed in correspondence with our advancing needs: as she is also the home of a definite disclosure of God, Who has communicated Himself to man, and revealed Himself in the person of His Son[1].

This idea of the Church, as one states it, seems most credible, most natural. The strength of its appeal to tradition, to the earliest traditions of many Churches, is undoubted. Its sanction, in the language of the New Testament, is hardly more open to question; while, once again, it is in conspicuous agreement with the needs of men, and with what one may call the principle of the Incarnation—the dignity which the Incarnation gives to material things. But there is no idea so true as not to admit of being abused. And, in fact, this Church idea has so degenerated at times into formalism, or materialism, or tyranny, as to account for, if not wholly to justify, reactions —reactions which are one-sided. It is only so that it could have come about—as conspicuously it has come about in our own country—that St. Paul's doctrine of Justification by Faith could be put into opposition to what is also

[1] See app. note 11.

St. Paul's own doctrine of Church and Sacraments[1], and identified with a party of its own, while it has been left to another less defined party to reiterate that all religion has after all no other end or test than the production of good living. What is it but a miserable and foolish one-sidedness that can ever have put these truths into antagonism one to another? For St. Paul's doctrine of Justification by Faith, what is it? It means that what justifies a man, or puts him into a relation of acceptance with God, is not anything material, or external, like circumcision, or any methodical observance of a prescribed rule like the Jewish Law, but something more true to man's fundamental dependence upon God; it is the surrender of man's being into the hand of God considered as making in Christ the simple offer of His love. Wearied with his efforts to justify himself, wearied with his own false independence, man at last, within or without the discipline of the Jewish Law, learns to find his true

[1] See Rom. vi. 3; Tit. iii. 5; Acts xix. 1-7; 1 Cor. x. 16; xi. 23-34; 2 Tim. i. 6.

peace in surrendering at discretion to God, and simply accepting the offer of His love. This is justifying faith; it establishes the right relation of the soul to God. But it is the beginning, not the end, of that relation. The man grows 'from faith to faith'; or (again in St. Paul's words) he 'has access by faith into that grace wherein' for the future 'he stands[1].' That is, the believing soul, whose simple surrender to God's promises has removed all the obstacles to his justification, is baptized in the 'bath of regeneration,' 'baptized into Christ.' He receives the Spirit, he enters into the communion of the body and blood of Christ. In this new position, the function of his faith is changed. Intellectually it dwells upon the person of the Redeemer, and passes from faith into knowledge; morally, it keeps hold of God who has apprehended the soul; also it becomes a perpetual correspondence with the movements of the Spirit whom it has received; a perpetual assimilation, manducation, appropriation of spiritual gifts.

[1] Rom. i. 17; v. 2.

Unity within the Church of England. 71

Christians in the New Testament are never regarded as persons who need to ask for the Spirit as if they had not already received Him; but they are called upon to stir up, to use the gift which is already in them, or to abstain from grieving the Spirit whom they already possess[1]. The function of faith in the Christian life is to draw upon or realize its existing resources.

But all this doctrine of faith is in no kind of antagonism to the doctrine of the Church and the sacraments, rightly understood. Everywhere life and growth consists in an appropriation by an organism of what is supplied to it from without. This holds good in the spiritual life. The Church is, in recent language, the environment of the soul, the sacraments constitute the external supply. The supply is real. The sacramental gifts are valid through the Spirit's action without any effort on our part. They are God's gifts simply. But their whole effect on us depends on the degree of assimilative and appropriative effort—the degree

[1] See app. note 12.

of faith—which we exercise. According to our faith is it done to us. This was the law of Christ's physical healings during His life on earth. The instrument of healing was the power or virtue which went out from His sacred person, but the effect in each case was dependent on the response of faith. Where there was no faith, there was no healing. According to their faith it was done to them. Their faith it was that made them whole. So it is with our Lord's work of spiritual re-creation now that He is at the right hand of God. The restorative power, of which His sacraments are the ordained channels, depends for its efficacy in each case (not for its reality, I say, but for its effect) on the response of faith. Nor is it that the gift from without is God's, and the response from within simply our own act. No! Within us and without it is the Spirit's action. From without He comes to us with gifts of grace in all the organized system of His Church: within us He works to quicken our coldness, and to overcome our wilfulness, till we exhibit the free and eager

Unity within the Church of England. 73

response of a converted heart to the offer of God. And all the external supply of grace, and all the inner response of faith, is but a means to that which is the only end of all religion—the renewal of the soul, of the whole man into the image of Him who created it.

Brethren, need we be for ever in reactions? Let us who believe profoundly in the sacraments see to it that we never let them, so far as lies in us, be spoken of, or treated, or used as charms. Let us give no countenance, for instance, to any use of baptism such as would allow children, who are not in immediate danger of death, to be baptized when there is no fair prospect of their being brought up to understand the meaning of their Christian vocation—a practice, I believe, utterly contrary to fundamental Christian principles [1]. Let us see to it that on our side there is no failure to preach the necessity of the faith which alone justifies, and of the converted will. Let us see to it that we never allow in our thoughts or our language any other measure of ecclesiastical success than

[1] See app. note 13.

the promotion of holiness, the promotion of goodness, in the actual lives of men. Let us see to it we are not one-sided; and then we may have better hopes of reunion among ourselves in our own Church of England. For to St. Paul the three aspects of truth which, more or less roughly, have been identified with three parties in our Church, are not opposites but correlatives. Three times he states the essence of the true religion in antithesis to the externalism of the Judaists, and three times in different terms. 'Circumcision,' he cries three times over[1], 'is nothing, and uncircumcision is nothing, but . . . . faith working by love.' Do you ask what is the essence of true religion viewed as the response of man to God? It is operative faith. And again '. . . . the keeping of the commandments of God.' Do you ask what is true religion considered in its end and fruit? It is actual conformity of our lives to the divine requirements. But once again '. . . . a new creature.' Do you ask what is the essence of true religion considered from the

[1] Gal. v. 6; vi. 15; 1 Cor. vii. 19.

side of God? It is that new creative act—the new creative act of grace—which in all its stages finds its expression in the Church, and its instruments in the sacraments. The system of grace, the response of faith, the result in obedience—brethren, these are not opposites; they are the correlatives the one of the other. They are all of the essence of the one spiritual religion.

IV.

Let me summarize the conclusions to which I have endeavoured to lead you.

1. The Church of England has certainly a dogmatic basis. Any one who would dissolve that basis of dogma—for example by suggesting that men should be admitted to the ministry who do not in simplicity of heart hold the Creed—is undermining thereby the basis of our religion as a whole; for our religion rests upon the word of God, the self-revelation of God incarnate in the person of Jesus Christ.

2. The Church of England insists upon a limited amount of dogma, and beyond that

admits a considerable degree of divergence of opinion. It seems to me very possible that this is the ideal of Church government;—that whilst it was necessary there should be certain definitions, and that the limits of Church communion should be laid down up to a certain point, possibly it was not desirable that exact definition should proceed far. In matters of ordinary civil government, we recognize that some external legislation is necessary, but over-legislation we think a bad thing. The same may be the ideal in Church government also. In any case it is the fact that the Church of England, in Creed, Catechism, and Articles, fairly interpreted, makes certain dogmatic claims; and beyond the point to which they extend admits of a considerable degree of divergent opinion.

3. Beyond the point to which the dogmatic requirement reaches we are still responsible; responsible for completeness of knowledge and of teaching. Each one of us starts with certain favourite doctrines and views of truth. There are parts of the Bible we like to read; parts

about which we feel uncomfortable. Starting with such predilections we are, I say, responsible for advancing, by prayer and efforts of spiritual apprehension, till those parts of truth least congenial to our nature are really appropriated. We are to put ourselves to school impartially at each of the books of the New Testament. We are to grow to an intelligent grasp upon the Catholic faith, and to remember that we are the merest slaves if we are satisfied with bare orthodoxy. What is actually prescribed is but the starting-point for spiritual apprehension.

4. The temper of theology ought to be the temper of appreciation. A great deal in life depends upon the temper of mind in which we approach the opinions of others; upon whether we endeavour to see as much good in them as possible, or, on the other hand, approach them in the attitude of criticism, to find what we can take hold of and find fault with. And of these two tempers of mind there is no doubt which is the more Christian; for 'the wisdom that is from above is first pure, then peaceable,

considerate, persuasible, full of mercy and good fruits, without partiality, and without hypocrisy. And the fruit of righteousness is sown in peace by them that make peace.'

LECTURE III.

THE RELATION OF THE CHURCH TO INDEPENDENT AND HOSTILE OPINION.

'Therefore, seeing we have this ministry, as we have received mercy we faint not. But have renounced the hidden things of dishonesty, not walking in craftiness, nor handling the word of God deceitfully; but by manifestation of the truth commending ourselves to every man's conscience in the sight of God.'—2 *Cor.* iv. 1, 2.

Reverend Father in God, my brethren of the clergy and of the laity,—We have been occupied in considering the divine mission of the Church as a whole, and the doctrinal basis on which we rest in the Church of England in particular; this afternoon we are to go on to consider the relation in which we stand towards independent or hostile forms of thought in the world without us.

What in general is to be our attitude towards opposition? Is it to be in the main an attitude of controversy? I answer, no. I remember when I was being ordained priest, the late Bishop of Oxford was interpreting to the candidates for ordination St. Paul's advice to Timothy and Titus—'Let no man despise thee,' 'let no man despise thy youth'; and he said this did not mean that we were to go about asserting ourselves everywhere, but that it did mean that we were to be the sort of men whom people could not despise. Now this lesson for the individual priest applies also to the Church. 'Let no man despise her.' This does not mean that she is to be towards all alien or independent societies in a perpetual attitude of controversy and self-assertion; but that living by her own proper principles, she is to be her true self, the sort of body, having for her representatives the sort of men, that people cannot despise. We must bear our witness, teach the truth committed to us, and do our duty; and certain it is that by teaching positively what we have to teach, and being positively what God means us to be, we shall find ourselves in the right relation towards hostile or alien modes of thought.

I.

We are to teach positively what we have to teach. On this some emphasis needs to be laid. One often hears alarming things said about the forces opposed to us. People get into a condition of panic and express their alarm by denunciation; but in fact, our strength lies in looking to our own household, and setting it in order. For example, one sometimes hears alarming things said about the progress of the Roman Church in England. I do not believe, in fact, that the Roman Church in England, as judged by its own statistics, can be said to advance. But, from time to time, you hear no doubt of people becoming Roman Catholics. Now when you inquire into such cases, or have the circumstances brought under your notice, you find generally that the cause of such secessions, at least among the laity, lies in our not having done our duty by them in the Church – in the Church of the place where they lived not having really shepherded them. Either the penitent soul was not quite frankly offered those opportunities of confession which the Prayer-book would desire that it should be given; or the anxious and inquiring spirit was not met with the advice and solicitude which it had a right to ask for. It was either that we clergy met some suggested 'difficulty' by ridicule or evasion, not being ourselves sufficiently equipped to give the advice or counsel needed, or that they of the laity had not, in fact, been instructed as they ought to have been in the case of which we have no kind of reason to be ashamed—the case, positive and negative, for the Church of England.

If you turn in another direction, and dwell upon the rise and progress of Nonconformity, there can be no question at all—it is, in fact, hardly questioned—that it was due in the past, not to any spirit of schism, but, at least in the great majority of instances, to the fact that the Anglican Church was not behaving as the true

Its relation to Independent Opinion. 83

mother of the people. You know this was the case in the Church of Wales. Let her become again but the true mother in Israel, and we may be quite sure that gradually—not at once, for evils of long standing are not rectified at once—the children will come to recognize their mother.

I say then that the prevalence of forms of thought or belief alien or hostile to the Church of England, is to lead us, first of all, to be more true to our own principles, and to teach with more positive plainness what the Church commissions us to teach. We are not to be denunciatory, but positive. But to be this involves a good deal of study, thought, and prayer. It is easy to indulge in vague denunciations in the pulpit; and easy again to give ourselves to general moral exhortation. Our people are given too much vague denunciation of what is, or is supposed to be, evil, and they are too much exhorted. What they need is to be taught positively, clearly, and scripturally. I am sure there is a danger at present that advance in the conduct of services, advance in ritual, should outrun the real advance in positive teaching. No one who is wise would undervalue reverent worship. I may remind you of the sentence of Hooker: 'Duties of religion performed by whole societies of men ought to have in them, according to our power, a sensible excellency correspondent to the majesty of him whom we worship.' Who could deny this? But there is a danger that solicitude about services should outrun solicitude about teaching, and that we should be over-easily satisfied with 'getting a good service.' Let me exemplify the lack of positive teaching in the matter of Holy Communion.

An exhortation to Communion is introduced constantly at the end of a sermon. But what is the use of such reiterated parenthetic exhortations? People will be ready enough to come to Communion if they understand what its inestimable benefits are. But in fact they do not understand the scope of the Eucharist as communion, as sacrifice, as worship. If they are to understand it, we must not be satisfied with a parenthetic reference, but must

Its relation to Independent Opinion. 85

supply thorough and systematic teaching. We ought to devote entire sermons to particular subjects, not selected in accordance with our own proclivities, but following impartially the order of teaching suggested by the Creed and Catechism, always supporting the teaching of the Church by constant and obvious reference to Holy Scripture—'teaching out of the Bible.' To do this involves study on our part. It is only by study that we can do our duty. And it is all-important that our teaching should be, not according to the partiality of the individual, but, fully and systematically, the whole of what the Church puts into our hands to teach. It has been one-sided teaching, or the neglect of parts of the truth, that has been in past history the excuse, if not the justification, for schisms.

We are, then, not to be primarily controversial; but to be occupied in positive teaching. And yet, without being controversial, we shall find ourselves in opposition to alien and hostile forms of thought of different sorts in different directions. Thus we must be combatants, for we are to 'try the spirits,' and 'even now in the world are there many antichrists.' Do not let us give way to effeminate complaints of the forces now opposed to us, talking about 'the good old times,' and contrasting them with the times in which we live; for, in fact, if there is one thing which history makes more certain than another, it is that there never were any good old times. Think, for example, of the circumstances of the apostolic age; think of the Epistles of St. John to the Seven Churches, or the Epistle of St. Jude, documents which belong to the end of the apostolic age and speak of the dangers which then threatened the Church. Were those good times? Or pass into the second century, and study the struggle against various forms of Gnosticism. Hear Celsus, from without, saying that Christianity was already split into so many sects that there was nothing in common among them but their name[1]; and Tertullian, from within, regretting that 'the

[1] Orig. *c. Cels.* iii. 12.

Its relation to Independent Opinion. 87

most faithful, the wisest, the most experienced in the Church were for ever going over to the wrong side ¹.' Were those good times? Or, the age of the Councils; the age to which we owe the Creeds, strong, clear, masterful formulas? That was an age of wild controversy; and, amid the din of jarring voices, people seemed hardly able to hear the notes of certain truth at all. That was not a 'good time.' How was it with the Middle Ages? People talk about the 'ages of faith.' Certainly, there was more credulity, more readiness to accept what was proclaimed on authority, whether true or false; but, so far as faith implies some moral effort, there is no reason to think that there was more of it than there is now. Read St. Bernard, and you will see he did not look on his times as good times. Once more, take the age of Bishop Butler. 'It is come,' he says, 'I know not how, to be taken for granted by many persons, that Christianity is not so much as a subject for inquiry; but that it is

¹ *De praescr.* 3.

now, at length, discovered to be fictitious. And, accordingly, they treat it as if in the present age this were an agreed point among all persons of discernment; and nothing remained but to set it up as a principal subject of mirth and ridicule, as it were by way of reprisals, for its having so long interrupted the pleasures of the world.' Were those good times? Or, take the generation immediately behind our own. A good old churchman who died not many years ago, used to protest, if he heard men of a younger generation complaining of the evils of the time: 'If you had been born when I was, you would wonder that there was any Church of England left.' It is the fact that in every age we have to struggle for a truth that seems hardly bestead.

II.

In this connection we ought to study more, perhaps, than we do the message of the Apocalypse. It is the book of the New Testament which conveys one particular lesson—the lesson that the Bride of Christ is for ever passing through those same phases of fortune that Christ in His human life passed through: the cause the same, the seeming defeat the same, the same the passage through the grave and gate of death to a joyful resurrection[1]. The Apocalypse lays down the main conditions and principles of our perpetual spiritual conflict. Under symbolical forms we have set before us the great drama and the *dramatis personæ*. On one side, the forces of God—God, Who sitteth upon His throne, the sovereign; and the Lamb, crucified and triumphant, God's revelation to men of the victory of meekness and self-sacrifice; and the seven Spirits before the throne, representing the universal, secret workings of God; and the Bride, the New Jerusalem, representing the true humanity, the true society, which God has been gathering, and which will be at last supreme. And, on the other side, symbolical forms of evil: 'The old serpent, called the Devil and Satan,' Satan setting himself up in opposition to God; and

[1] Rev. xi. 7-12.

the great Beast, the beast of violence and persecution, the counterpart of the meek Lamb who yields Himself to sacrifice, and through sacrifice triumphs; and over against the seven Spirits the second Beast, the beast who represents the deceitfulness of sin, the spirit of worldliness and false philosophy; and over against the Bride, the New Jerusalem, the woman, the harlot, representing false human society, whose characteristics are gathered from all corrupt forms of civilization with which the Bible presents us, Sodom, Babylon, Egypt, Rome—the persecuting empire of Rome—and, Jerusalem, the apostate Church, rejecting and crucifying Christ. These 'persons' of the spiritual drama are exhibited to us in conflict, and the spectacle of conflict passes into that of the divine victory. And the whole succession of spectacles teaches us the conditions of our own present struggle—the nature of the antagonism we are to expect, and the weapons of conflict which we are to use, and the issue which lies before us. Sometimes evil will present itself in the form of persecution; sometimes with 'the deceitfulness of sin,' no longer as the lion, but as the adder, in the subtle influences of worldliness and disbelief. And the method of defence— the method of the Lamb and His martyrs— is to be the method of mingled loyalty and meekness. We are to be like Christ, who rode out because of the word of truth and righteousness, but truth and righteousness linked by meekness. Only through meekness can we triumph; truth and righteousness not linked by meekness can never represent the cause of Christ. In the spirit of Christ's meekness we are to bear witness, to bear witness (if it be so) even unto death, and in the confidence of His resurrection to look forward to the certain issue. For the kingdoms of the world are to become the kingdom of the Lord and of His Christ. Through the grave and gate of death the Church passes to her triumph.

III.

We are to bear our witness, then, as Churchmen, in the face of alien and hostile forms of thought. Let us consider this—to-day only as concerns our witness to theological truth; for the consideration of our moral witness we will reserve for to-morrow—first as it affects us at home, and secondly with reference to the mission field. First, as it affects us at home. And whilst it is impossible to survey in any sense the whole field, I would call your attention to four points on which, it seems to me, we are especially called to maintain our witness at the present crisis of thought.

1. We are to bear witness to the principle of faith. People in many directions are disposed to disparage faith, and to complain of its being required of them. The complaint is in the air: it influences men almost without their knowing it. They have an idea that it is 'unreasonable to believe what cannot be proved.' It is not unreasonable. And in vindicating the principle of faith it is of great importance that it should be set in antithesis not to reason but to sight. The popular antithesis of faith and reason is a very dangerous one, and it is unscriptural. In the New Testament faith is opposed always

to sight, never to reason; and the difference is significant. 'Faith is the evidence (or test) of things not seen.' Faith is the faculty in us by which we pass out beyond present experience, and lay hold upon eternal realities and grounds of confidence.

But this faculty for going beyond present experience is a faculty of our reason. It is in order to be rational—that is, in order to give rational account of the world and our own nature, in order to realize all that our nature is capable of—it is in order to be rational that we travel beyond what we can see and are brought, more or less fully, into contact with God and eternity.

The principle of faith is brought into exercise to some extent in all human life and knowledge. Thus the ultimate postulates and principles on which physical science depends—such as the unity of all things, the universality of law, the persistence of force—these are not truths that can be proved. They are assumptions that science is bound to make[1]. Thus there is

[1] See app. note 14.

something akin to faith necessary in the very beginnings of scientific inquiry. But its necessity is much more apparent in social relations. Human life is based on the principle of faith. You must go far beyond what you can prove as to people's trustworthiness; you must trust the instinct of sonship and brotherhood. And speaking generally you find your trust justified. On the whole, 'according to our faith, so is it done to us.' The man who goes furthest in believing in humanity is the man who draws most out of it, whilst the most sceptical and cynical is most often deceived. In the sphere of personal morality the requirement of faith is still more apparent. If we would be moral we must throw ourselves upon the right, in the supreme confidence that what ought to be can be. And faith is only finding its true home and justification when it goes one step further on and realizes its personal relation to God. For 'unto Thyself, O God, hast thou made us, and unquiet is our heart until it rest on Thee.' Still our faith is rational. It is not without reason that we believe. God has not left Himself without witness in nature and conscience; still more in Jesus Christ. But witness is not demonstration. We need the venture of faith to 'see him who is invisible.' Our Lord develops this faculty in His disciples—our Lord who is the Master of our true humanity. He, I say, whilst giving the disciples grounds for believing in Himself, and in the Father through Him, does obviously encourage and develop in them the faculty of faith. We then are not to be ashamed of it, or apologize for it, as if it were unreasonable. Nor, inasmuch as it is the noblest of our faculties, shall we be surprised if its exercise is sometimes difficult. It is hard, as it is supremely noble, to 'endure as seeing him who is invisible.' It would not be worth all it is worth if it was not often difficult to believe. Nor is it, any more than any other truly human faculty, a power which we can exercise without God's help. 'No man can say (or continue to say) that Jesus is Lord but by the Holy Ghost.' Faith is difficult then, and a habit which requires divine assistance; but it is rational. It is rational, I say, because it and it alone enables us to give a rational account of all the facts of the world, of all that science and history discloses, and also of all that lies hid, half realized, half concealed, in the depths of our own being; of all that spiritual men have shown our humanity to be capable of in sonship to God. Faith enables us to move through the whole world of nature and of man as those who have the clue to its secrets; who are at home in it; who are 'not afraid of any evil tidings, for their heart standeth fast, trusting in the Lord.' Indeed the spirit of Christian sonship is the only true rationality.

2. We are to bear witness to the Being of God, and that in an intellectual atmosphere which, under the influence of a school of scientific enquirers, exhibits some tendency towards Agnosticism—that is, the denial that we can know of the existence of God at all, or anything about Him. We maintain, then, in the face of this tendency, that we have grounds for knowing—in part knowing, and in part believing—*that* God is, and *what* He is.

Ought it to distress us that we should find ourselves confidently affirming what the representatives of physical science—that is, the representatives of the branches of knowledge in which the greatest recent advances have been made—not seldom deny? I answer, on the whole, no: in part because the agnosticism of men of science is exaggerated; and when they are, as very many of them are, earnest believers, their freedom in the facts of science is not one whit diminished by their Christian faith. In part because it is a fact conspicuous in the history of mankind that, whereas the representatives of great intellectual movements at different epochs have interpreted truly the movement which they represented in itself, they have been strangely blind to the place which it was destined to hold in the whole of human knowledge or human life.

Thus the great Greek philosophers interpreted truly Greek institutions, and estimated aright their positive value, but were blind in thinking these institutions final and the last word of social progress in the world. The representatives of the Roman empire, again, knew the real dignity and value of that empire, but were blind to the relative place it would hold by the side of its despised contemporary the Christian Church. The Reformers, once again, had real truth on their side; there were real principles which they were vindicating, real abuses against which they were protesting; but how extraordinarily blind, speaking generally, were the Reformers to the sum of positive religious forces with which they had to reckon. What a surprise to them would the religious history have been which links their time with ours! They were as blind surely to the forces of Catholicism as were the Deists of the last century to the real if dormant strength of supernatural Christianity. Once again, and for the last time, the Radical reformers of the earlier part of this century set their minds on certain reforms which are now practically accomplished. They estimated rightly the necessity and the possibility of the reforms they advocated; but how short-sighted they were as to the good that would be effected in human life as a whole by the mere external enfranchisement of individual action.

I learn then from past experience that I must attend with great respect to the positive teaching in their own department of any body of men who represent with tolerable unanimity a great advance in knowledge or power. I must attend with great respect to the scientific teaching of scientific men. But I shall not anticipate that representatives of one particular movement are likely to estimate rightly the place it will take in the whole of human life. Thus I shall not listen with the same respect to the representatives of science when they pass from teaching science to denouncing theology or depreciating religion. Those inside a movement cannot generally see sufficiently clearly what lies outside it. Those whose interests are less specialized are more likely to estimate the place it will take in the whole of human life.

We must regret, I think, that theologians were unduly slow to recognize the vast amount of evidence on which reposes the scientific theory of evolution through natural selection.

But in proportion as people lose their fear of it and come to accept it, they will surely perceive that the claim made for it by agnosticism, the claim that it enables us to account for the development of the world without postulating throughout the action of mind, is an altogether exaggerated claim; it is altogether to overestimate the function of natural selection [1].

Science has, in fact, taught us a great deal as to the method of creation—how continuous it has been, how gradual, how even tentative—but it has done nothing at all to explain the origin of force, of matter, of life, nothing at all to dissolve the conviction which belongs to the rational mind of man, that this world of universal order and law and beauty, this world which 'while it works as a machine also sleeps as a picture,' is the work of mind and spirit like ours—mind and spirit which is the vast whole of which ours is but the tiny product or reflection.

3. We are to maintain a historical religion—a historical revelation of God in Christ; and this in face of a destructive criticism.

[1] See app. note 15.

In the Church Congress in this diocese last year you had a discussion of the Church's gains from Biblical criticism. The discussion dealt almost entirely with criticism as applied to the Old Testament. Now criticism as applied to the Old Testament presents us at present with a great many unsolved problems and some fairly certain conclusions which seem to demand rather unexpected changes in our conception of the literary character of some of the books, and of the process by which they took their present shape. That subject was dealt with from this place at large and very ably by Professor Kirkpatrick last year[1]. We need not suppose, as his lectures sufficiently indicate, that the change of position ultimately required of us will be such as the extremists among critics would desire. The existing evidence in fact points in two directions. If, on the one hand, literary analysis emphasizes the composite character of the 'books of Moses,' and historical enquiry enforces the belief that the Mosaic law was

[1] *The Divine Library of the Old Testament* (Macmillan, 1891).

the result of a gradual process of development and centralization; on the other hand, oriental archaeology discloses the existence of the knowledge of writing, and considerable development of literary skill, both in Palestine and Egypt, a century before the Exodus. Such discoveries as those at Tel-el-amarna make it easy to suppose that some written law and written records go back among the Jews to the period of Moses [1].

Certain changes, however, will be required of us. We must remember, as St. Augustine has expressed it, that, if it be wronging the Old Testament to deny that it comes from the same God as the New, on the other hand, it is wronging the New Testament if the Old is placed on a level with it. The Old Testament represents the gradual method by which God led men on, 'in many parts and many manners' through a process of education preparing the way for Christ. The meaning of the Old

---

[1] On this subject, and on the questions connected with Old Testament criticism generally, I have endeavoured to speak more at length in *Lux Mundi* (John Murray, 12th ed. 1891), pp. 247 ff. and Pref. to 10th ed.

Testament is to be sought in the partial witness which each book bears to the central truth of the Incarnation.

Now it seems to me unfortunate that the discussions at your Church Congress dealt so disproportionately with the Old Testament. For surely, when we are thinking of our 'gains from Biblical criticism,' our attention is more naturally directed in the first instance to the New Testament. Surely, it is here that our gains are most conspicuous. Those who are alarmed at the tendencies of Old Testament criticism, sometimes ask where it will stop, whether it will not go on to the New Testament. But, in fact, such a question shows an ignorance of the situation. Criticism began with the New at least as soon as with the Old Testament. The New Testament documents have been sifted by the most thorough criticism which can be conceived; and, so far from having been invalidated, they stand in a stronger position than that in which they stood fifty years ago, in proportion as the examination has been more thorough.

Trace back the Synoptic Gospels to the two primitive documents which so many critics postulate—the original collection of discourses represented in St. Matthew, and the original narrative of events represented in St. Mark's Gospel. When you consider the Christ depicted in these, do you find that you have got any nearer to a merely 'natural' or human Christ, to one who by gradual accretion was raised into a supernatural figure? No: the fundamental narrative of events is permeated by miracles which resist all attempts to explain them away; and the original collection of discourses represents in all its unmistakable force the strictly divine claim of our Lord. Investigation, again, shows us at the very roots of St. Paul's teaching the doctrine of the Incarnation, as a matter not in dispute, any more than the fact of the resurrection, between him and the Judaizers. Investigation once again leaves the strength of the evidence on the side of the authenticity of the fourth Gospel. And, as Professor Sanday has very recently said, 'we cannot help being reminded that scarcely one of

Its relation to Independent Opinion. 105

the discoveries of recent years has not had for its tendency to bring back the course of criticism into paths nearer to those marked out by ancient tradition [1].' Certainly historical evidence is not generally demonstrative, and the historical title-deeds of our faith do not appear to be intended to force conviction upon any man's mind; but they do support it and justify it. I am sure that I am within the mark in saying that in view of recent criticism of the New Testament, it is those who deny and not those that affirm the faith of the Church who do violence to the evidence [2].

There are other issues, even in the new Testament, which are secondary and less decisive. But in regard to the central facts on which our historical religion depends, the historical witness stands with unimpeachable strength. We are not then to go about decrying criticism. We are to invite criticism to do all it can, and ask only for justice.

[1] See *Two Present Day Questions* (Longmans, 1892), p. 37.
[2] See this argument at greater length in *Bampton Lectures*, 1891 (Murray), Lect. III.

We must remember further that our historical religion—our religion which looks back to a disclosure of God, through a historical incarnation, in the person of Jesus Christ—gives us another great advantage as rational men. The doctrine of the triune being of God, which is unmistakably involved in our Lord's language about His relation to the Father and the Holy Ghost—this doctrine of the triune being enables us to maintain a rational Theism. Theism requires us to think of God as an independent, eternal, spiritual Being. Indeed there is an end to the humility or reality of religion if God is thought to depend upon us in order to have some one to know and to love. But you cannot think of an independent, eternal, spiritual life in God, if the being of God is blank and monotonous unity. The life of spirit, the life of will and knowledge and love, involves relationship. For love there must be a lover and a loved; for thought there must be a thinker and an object of thought; for fruitful will there must be the perpetual passage of will into effect. And it is thus the doctrine of the Trinity, though we could not have invented or discovered it for ourselves, which makes our thought of God rational and real, because it shows us God not in isolation, but in perpetual fellowship within Himself. The eternal being of the Father passes out into its adequate self-expression in the eternal Word or Son; and the Father in the Son knows Himself and loves Himself; and the fellowship of the Father and the Son finds its perfection in the Holy Ghost who is the eternal product and joy of both.

We are to maintain, then, the historical Christ as the disclosure of God to us, and as the foundation of an intelligible Theism [1].

4. Lastly, have we not need to maintain 'the Gospel' in view of reactions against what is called 'old-fashioned Evangelical Christianity?' This old-fashioned Evangelicalism, dealt almost exclusively with the doctrine of atonement and the vicarious aspects of Christianity. And these were preached in a way that did violence to the moral sense of mankind. There has

[1] See *Bampton Lectures*, Lect. V.

come, and rightly, a great reaction; but it appears to be imagined in some quarters that we are almost to abandon the preaching of the doctrine of atonement and of the vicarious aspect of Christianity, confining ourselves to the doctrine of the Incarnation and its extension in the sacraments of the Church. Now nothing that has taken such hold of the human heart as the doctrine of atonement could ever pass into oblivion. It may have been put into undue prominence, and we must rectify the balance; but no more. There are two elements in the Gospel: there is first, Christ *for* us—our example, our sacrifice, God's simple gift to us from outside; and, secondly, Christ *in* us, renewing our lives inwardly by His Spirit into union with His own.

Now it is not a question of whether we shall preach the one or the other of these elements in the Gospel. If we would be true to the New Testament, we must preach and hold them both. For it is Christ in us that makes intelligible Christ for us; and it is Christ for us who prepares the way for Christ in us. It is Christ for us in awful solitude 'treading the wine-press alone' who lives the true human life and offers the perfect human sacrifice to the divine righteousness. This is God's gift to us which, in utter repudiation of any merits of our own, we are simply to accept in faith. But Christ can thus act 'for us' because He proceeds to act 'in us.' His Spirit comes forth out of His ascended and glorified manhood and links us on to Him; henceforth it is Christ in us imparting His life to us and identifying us with Himself. If then we are to bear a complete witness, if we are to appeal to the consciences of men both as they desire pardon for sin and as they desire actual righteousness, we shall not preach one or other of these elements in the Gospel, but the truth of both.

Here are four ways in which our witness is required—as to the principle of faith: as to the being of God: as to His revelation of Himself in the historical person of Jesus Christ and the events of His human life: as to the full meaning of the Gospel which is embodied in Christ's person, our sacrifice as well as our example and our new life.

IV.

I have left myself but little time to speak of the witness which the Church must bear abroad among the heathen. It is the same witness but under different conditions—in face of Hindu, Buddhist, Mohammedan forms of thought, in India, China, Japan, and the region of the Turkish Empire lost to the Church, and in face of less developed forms of belief among less civilized tribes. Not nearly half of the world, we must remember, is yet Christian. It is the catholic mission and claim of the Church that we are called upon to vindicate. This means that Christ is adequate for all races, and can satisfy all forms of human need. Already in the history of Christianity it has appeared how each fresh race as it has been brought within the Church, has both itself found its sanctification there, and also has brought out some fresh aspect of the full meaning of Christ. It was but a very small part of Christianity which

Its relation to Independent Opinion. 111

emerged in the purely Jewish Church. The Greek race, with its unique powers of intellect, had for its vocation to bring out the treasures of wisdom which lay hid in Christ. To it in the main we owe our theology. The Roman race, with its wonderful powers of discipline and organization, built up the mediaeval Papacy, that glorious witness to the governing and disciplining forces of Christianity. The Teutonic race has surely taught the world much that it would not otherwise have known, of the power of Christianity in consecrating individual character. And there still remain great and rich gifts for consecration; the subtilty of the Hindus, the patience of the Chinese, the geniality and gentleness of the Japanese. Here are great qualities not yet, except in small measure, sanctified in Christ; and we shall not see the full glory of Christianity till these alien races are brought inside the circle of the Church, to bring unsuspected treasures of wisdom and beauties of character out of the same old and unchanging creed.

Such considerations may fire our imaginations: but, prior to them and more simply cogent there lies upon us the injunction of Christ—'Go ye into all the world,' 'make disciples of all the nations, baptizing them into the name of the Father, and of the Son, and of the Holy Ghost.'

Brethren, here then is our paramount duty. It is a shame how long, to how wide an extent, with what disastrous results, we have forgotten it. We are to proclaim Christianity as superseding all other religions by a method not so much of exclusion as of inclusion. For Christ 'the light which lighteneth every man,' the Word in every man's heart, has left Himself nowhere, in no religion, without witness. All religions contain more or less considerable elements of truth. And Christianity, I say, supersedes other religions by including the elements of truth which belong to each in a vaster and completer whole. It supersedes them as daylight supersedes twilight; aye, makes the twilight by comparison to be as the night. In part then it is by direct opposition to what is positively evil, in part by sympathetic re-

Its relation to Independent Opinion. 113

cognition of the elements of truth in alien systems, that we have to bear our witness in heathen countries.

And when we think of it, do we not, many of us, find ourselves in the wrong in this matter? Do we not need to have it more on our consciences, and in our prayers, to take more pains to interest our parishioners in some particular mission and to see that they know all about it? Nay more; do we not need to ask ourselves whether it may not be our own privilege to offer ourselves for foreign mission work? There can be no question that there are a vast number of divine vocations to this work missed, simply because people never trouble themselves to ask whether they may not themselves be called upon to do it. Can I then show cause why I should not be a missionary?

Brethren, in the Apocalypse there is set before us the picture of the perfected Church. It is completely catholic—'a great multitude which no man could number, of all nations and kindreds and people and tongues'; it is absolutely one—'the city that lieth four-square,' and from within its walls goes up the harmony of perfected praise. Again, it is wholly pure; the Bride of Christ, in white raiment, the perfected righteousnesses of the saints. Lastly it is triumphant and acknowledged of all, as 'the kings of the earth bring their glory and honour into it.' Catholic, one, pure, triumphant—we shall behold her, but not now; we shall see her, but not nigh. It is the vision of heaven, but it is the hope of earth. Meanwhile the vision is for an appointed time; and though it tarry we are to wait for it and to have it constantly in view. It is certain, that joy towards which we move. There is certain triumph before the cause of Christ. Conscious of this, we are to bear our witness, to suffer and to endure. It is hard to go on patiently to the end of life without letting our ideal fade and vanish; and yet it is herein that Christianity lies. And for such as endure, as bear their witness to truth faithfully and fully in suffering and amidst opposition to the end, we know the reward. 'Ye are they who have continued with me in my temptations; and inasmuch as my Father appointed a kingdom unto me, I appoint unto you to eat and drink at my table in my kingdom; and ye shall sit on thrones, judging the twelve tribes of Israel[1].'

[1] St. Luke xxii. 29, 30.

LECTURE IV.

THE MISSION OF THE CHURCH IN SOCIETY.

> 'For the which cause I put thee in remembrance that thou stir up (stir into flame) the gift of God, which is in thee through the laying on of my hands. For God gave us not a spirit of fearfulness; but of power and love, and discipline.'—2 *Tim.* i. 6, 7 [R.V.].

Reverend Father in God, my brethren of the clergy, and of the laity,—We are to consider the Mission of the Church in Society: its mission to teach men moral and social principles by which they are to live according to the mind of Christ.

I.

If you read consecutively the Pastoral Epistles, you will be struck with the extent to which St. Paul conceives it to be the function of Timothy and Titus to be moral rulers. And this kingly office in the Church means not only, or chiefly, that we are to teach people to be true to their consciences, but even more, that we are to inform their consciences. For the cause of our unsatisfactory moral condition is not only that men do not do what they know to be right, but that they have so imperfect a moral ideal. God has endowed men with a perception, more or less instinctive, that they must do the right. But their knowledge of what the right is—their 'conscientia'—is not instinctive. It requires informing. Thus in fact you find infinite variety in the moral standards of mankind: and that because God has left it as the responsibility of men to inform their consciences according to the different degrees of opportunity which in different ages He has given them.

Now we Christians have a perfect standard set before us. We have the opportunities of thorough moral knowledge. Thus our responsibility as Christians is to keep our own consciences enlightened; and our responsibility as teachers is to enlighten the consciences of others. But this leaves us a great deal to do. What strikes us, I repeat, in nominally Christian society is not so much that people do not follow their consciences, as that they are so frequently deficient in moral knowledge, and more than this, blind to the responsibility they are under of keeping their consciences responsive to the word of God.

When we look back over history we wonder at the slackness of men's consciences in the past on points which seem to us clear enough. We examine the instruments of torture in some old house of the Inquisition, and marvel how men could ever have been so blind to the spirit of Christianity as to tolerate religious persecution at all, or, in particular, such methods of persecution. Or, to come to times nearer our own, we profess the greatest astonishment that members of our Houses of Parliament should have allowed themselves to accept bribes almost without concealment, as in fact the history of the last century records that they did. Or we read the history of the Church in Wales, in the sadly recent days when bishops were constantly non-resident, and we can hardly conceive how such a standard of conscience as to spiritual duties could ever have prevailed. We wonder at the blindness of the consciences of men in past times; but we forget that, unless we are very careful, we are in danger of exactly the same blindness, and that perhaps on points to which the mediæval conscience or the conscience of the past century was more sensitive than ours. At any rate it is a constant law of moral deterioration, as applicable to ourselves as to men of other ages, that conscience sinks to the level of practice.

It is not pleasant to mention particular points on which our conscience to-day seems to need re-adjustment to the standard of Christ, but I can hardly evade the necessity. Thus it seems to me a conspicuous instance of moral blindness, that people should fail to see that in investing their money they make themselves — within reasonable limits, but really—responsible for the use to which their money is put: that to put one's money, or allow it to be put, into any 'concern' without enquiry into the moral or social tendency of the concern, is to serve mammon at the expense of Christ. We cannot, in fact, hedge off any department of our life, and conduct it on what we call 'purely commercial principles' without reference to moral considerations. The 'mammon of unrighteousness,' the money that has been too long appropriated to unrighteous uses, has to be used by the servant of Christ to make to himself friends for eternity—in view therefore of eternal interests. In buying and selling, as in other respects, we are to 'seek first the kingdom of God.' And no one can tell what a difference it would make in the commercial world if it was known that the ears of Christians were alert to the calls of justice—that they would at once recognize it as their duty to refuse their support to any business the conduct of which involved oppression or unfairness.

Let me take quite a different instance. How extraordinarily blind are multitudes of Church people, in the highest not one whit less than in the lowest classes, to their responsibility for the religious education of their children, for seeing that their children really are instructed in those matters which form the contents of the Church Catechism, and in Holy Scripture.

It would not be hard to multiply instances of a defective conscience; but it is enough to notice these two, in which we seem to have fallen below the standard of past Christian ages. Who, I ask, could read the New Testament for the first time and imagine that Christian people, the people who profess to follow the teaching contained in it, could be indifferent on the points which I have mentioned?

II.

How then and on what authority are we to seek to instruct men's consciences on the Christian moral law? That law has, in principle, been laid down for us by our Lord in the Sermon on the Mount and elsewhere, and the New Testament is full of comments on this moral law of Christ. Further, you find that the Church was plainly invested by our Lord with the power of re-applying, from age to age, this moral law to the varying needs and circumstances of different generations. In other words, our Lord endowed the Church with the power of binding and loosing. He gave this power to the Church in the person of the representative apostle Peter; He recognized it also in the community as a whole[1]. In what different senses the power inheres in the Church and in the apostolic ministry we are not now concerned to enquire. We can be satisfied with the fact which lies plainly on the surface of Holy Scripture: the Church was endowed with this power of binding and loosing.

And there is no doubt what this means, because binding and loosing were perfectly well-known terms in our Lord's day. They were terms used of the Rabbis or Jewish masters. To bind was to prohibit a thing; to loose was to allow a thing. A strict Rabbi was said to 'bind,' or forbid, what a Rabbi of a laxer school would 'loose' or allow[2].

Our Lord then endowed the Church with

---

[1] St. Matt. xvi. 19; xviii. 18.
[2] See Edersheim, *Jesus the Messiah* (Longmans, 2nd ed.), ii. p. 85.

this legislative and judicial power to bind and loose; and though, no doubt, behind all mistakes of the Church there lies the corrective justice of God, which He never can surrender out of His own hands, yet the Church was intended to exercise this power, and that with a spiritual or supernatural sanction. 'Whatsoever ye shall bind on earth shall be bound in heaven; and whatsoever ye shall loose on earth shall be loosed in heaven.' In a word, the Church in every age is to apply or re-apply with a spiritual or supernatural sanction the religious and moral truth which our Lord intended to be for all time the basis of her life.

On the basis of this moral legislation, there was to be a moral discipline which is expressed in the absolving and retaining of sins[1]. The Church was to decide who could and who could not be admitted to baptism, to that 'baptism for the remission of sins,' which is the primary absolution. And when persons who had been baptized were guilty of notorious breaches of the Christian law, they were to be excluded

[1] St. John xx. 23.

from the privilege of the Christian society—there was to be a 'retaining' of their sins; and again, when the Church was satisfied of their repentance, a re-admission to the Christian status, or a renewed 'absolution.' So the Church was to exercise a disciplinary authority over her members. We can see examples of this authority in exercise plainly enough in the New Testament. Thus in the fifteenth chapter of the Acts of the Apostles we have an instance of how the Church exercised the binding and loosing power when circumstances required it, 'loosing' the gentile converts on the question of circumcision, whilst she 'bound' them on certain other points, on the eating of things strangled and things offered to idols; and on a sin conspicuously associated with idolatry, the sin of fornication. Or again we see the disciplinary authority applied to a person in the case of the incestuous man at Corinth. The Corinthian Christians, in what we may call the spirit of weak good-nature, were disposed to tolerate the sinner and his sin in their society. St. Paul sternly rebukes them.

The Mission of the Church in Society.

He tells them that while it is not the Christian function to 'judge those that are without,' they were bound to exercise judgment upon those within. Thus he requires them to exclude the offender from the Christian communion, until—as we seem to find in the Second Epistle—he had exhibited marks of true repentance; and then, 'lest he be swallowed up with over-much sorrow,' he desires him to be received back, and he himself admits him. 'To whom ye forgive anything, I forgive also: for if I forgave anything, to whom I forgave it, for your sakes forgave I it in the person of Christ[1].' The Christian society, then, is constantly to enunciate and re-apply the moral law, and to exercise discipline on the basis of this law; to exclude from fellowship those who are notoriously living in violation of it, and to re-admit them to fellowship when they again show themselves worthy of it.

III.

How is it that such obvious principles of the Christian society have fallen into abeyance?

[1] 1 Cor. v; 2 Cor. ii. 5-11.

I would point to two main causes of this disorder.

1. The first is to be sought in the history of penitential discipline in the middle ages. At first this discipline had been exercised in part publicly, in part privately; later on, for sufficiently obvious reasons, it became generally private. Still later, this private confession was made compulsory after having been voluntary for many centuries. In being made compulsory, its moral level was necessarily lowered. As a result of this lowering of the moral level of penitence, casuistry—which means the application of the general moral law to particular cases—came to be almost entirely what it ought not to have been—a negative thing; not an enunciation of how Christ would have men act, or of what Christians ought to do; but rather an attempt to minimize the moral requirement, to reduce it to its lowest possible terms, to find the easiest possible basis on which the priest could give absolution to the penitent. It was but a step from this that casuistry should become, what the casuistry of the Jesuits had in great

measure become when Pascal exposed it in his incomparable *Lettres Provinciales*, an evasion of the plain moral requirement of God in order to keep slack consciences within the communion of the Church.

2. But the cause of the decay of moral discipline in our own Church has been a different one —the peculiar relation in which the Church stands to the State, a relation which demands a word of explanation.

As you look at the New Testament, you see, without doubt, that the Church and the State are both divine institutions. The ministers of State are called God's ministers[1], as the ministers of the Church are called God's ministers. Both are divine institutions, but they exist on different planes, and for different objects; the State to be the minister of justice in the society of men generally; the Church to be the minister to the sons of faith of the fuller and deeper blessings included in Christ's redemption.

Subsequent history has shown how difficult

[1] Rom. xiii. 1-6.

is the adjustment of the relations of these two societies. At first they were obviously independent; and Christians had no doubt at all about the duty of recognizing that the powers of civil society, 'pagan' as it was, were ordained of God. On the other hand, civil society—that is, the Roman Empire—came to look suspiciously upon the Christian Church, an 'imperium in imperio' as it seemed to be, and in the age of persecution attempted to stamp it out by mere violence. We know how that attempt failed. The tables were turned. Later on, in the great days of the Papacy, we become witnesses of the rival attempt to reduce the State into subordination to the Church. Again the attempt failed. The obvious logic of facts was too much for the theory of the papal sovereignty on which it was based. There follows another attempt,, which had its chief expression in England, and especially at the period of the Reformation, the attempt to regard the Church and the State as in fact the same society in different aspects. Such a theory has found its noblest expression in the pages of Hooker. At bottom it rests upon the assumption that, inasmuch as the State is committed to Christian principles, the Church can go far towards merging herself in the State, and, in great measure, allow her administrative independence to be taken from her in return for national position.

It was a noble ideal; but an ideal on which subsequent events have cast a sinister light. To how small an extent can it be said that the English monarchy or nation has held itself bound by the principles of the Church. We live now under democratic influences. The law of the State depends on the will of the majority of the nation. What likelihood is there that the will of the majority should submit itself to the law of Christ? And if it be unlikely, what right had the Church to hamper her liberty to express and enforce by moral discipline on her own members the unchanging law of Christ?

In fact, it has come about that the English State law, as for example by the Divorce Act, has traversed the law of Christ. And the calamitous thing is this—that in nominally Christian society, there is extraordinarily little apprehension of the fact that, as Christians, men are under another law besides the law of the State. They are citizens, and as citizens they are bound to obey the State law in what belongs to State law; but they are Christians also, and as Christians they are bound to obey another law, the law of the Church; and it is no excuse for them, as Christians, that the law of the State does not enforce the law of Christ. They will be judged as Christians by the Christian law.

It is, then, at the present moment one main duty of the English Church to recall to the mind of her own members, and so to the minds of others, that there is an authority committed to her which is fundamentally independent of the functions and authority of the State; that, in the last issue, the duty of teaching and guarding the principles of Christian doctrine, discipline, and worship, was committed by Christ to one divine society, the Church; and not to that other divine society, with separate functions, the State.

IV.

In view of the situation and perils which I have now described, we have, I think, two obvious duties over and above the general reassertion of the ecclesiastical principle:—

1. We must get people to recognize the principle of Christian moral discipline. It is a plain fact, that Christ enunciated unchanging moral principles. The laws of men, the opinions of society, the policies of statesmen, all may change; but the mind of Christ for His disciples does not change. He is 'the same yesterday, to-day, and for ever.' And it is by the principles which He once for all enunciated that He will judge the world. We have to get men to recognize this. And in proportion as this is recognized, will there arise the possibility of legitimate Christian discipline. This revival of Christian discipline on the basis of the moral law is a hard thing to accomplish—nay, it may appear impossible, but diligent voluntary effort can, I believe, accomplish it. Think what voluntary effort has done in the last fifty

years in the revival of theology. Whether you approve or do not approve of the Tractarian revival you can learn one great lesson from it; you can learn the almost boundless power of a voluntary combination of Christian men profoundly in earnest. The circumstances looked hopeless enough for the revival of definite Church doctrine when the Tractarians began their work; but, as a matter of fact, that voluntary combination has accomplished to a surprising degree and in spite of crushing disasters what it desired. Dr. Pusey in his old age used to look back on the history of his life, with all its vicissitudes, and sum up his experience in the words of the Psalmist: 'Thanks be to God that he hath not cast out my prayer, nor turned his mercy from me.' Now we want a similar sort of voluntary combination for the assertion of the moral law of Christianity, and the restoration of that discipline, which is, I believe, a necessary part of the healthy life of any Christian society. No Christian society can be healthy unless there is some obvious means by which those acting in open defiance of Christian law shall forfeit, not the privileges of citizenship, but the privileges of Christian communion.

2. In order to this end we need to formulate anew, to apply anew, Christian morality: for the principles which by word and example our Lord laid down for His Church need constant re-application in view of new circumstances. We want a new casuistry, which will not be a statement of the minimum requirement, but an exposition of how Christians ought to act in the different departments of social life. This new casuistry will need to be formulated by voluntary effort in the first place, and might afterwards be taken into consideration by the authorities in the Church.

I will endeavour to specify some particular departments of life in which the Christian moral law needs to be reapplied or at least reasserted.

First, then, in regard to the indissolubleness of the marriage tie. Here it is true we are not without quite recent guidance. The last

Pan-Anglican Conference, leaving open one disputed point, laid down a certain number of clear principles[1]. Here then something still needs to be done in the way of enunciating the law; and, when this is done, we want every Churchman to understand clearly what the Christian marriage law is, and that it is the law for Christian men and women, not merely as individuals in private life, but as members of the Christian society, who are bound to 'judge' their fellows in respect of it so long as they are claiming to be members of the Church of Christ[2].

And, secondly, in regard to commercial morality. That is a matter of much more delicacy and difficulty. We know that a great deal contrary to Christian honesty, contrary to the laws of charity and brotherhood among classes, goes on in the commercial world. And as Christian teachers we are deterred from speaking out on the subject not only by fear of offending, but by a worthier motive—the fear of speaking ignorantly on a matter

---

[1] See app. note 16.   [2] 1 Cor. v. 12, 13.

The Mission of the Church in Society. 135

on which ignorant invective is sure to do a great deal of harm. We want then to organize on these matters all enlightened Christian opinion. The first step to this is to form small consultative bodies of men who know exactly what life means in workshops, in different business circles, among employers of labour, among workmen; they must be men who combine a profound practical Christianity with thorough knowledge of business ways. Such men could supply really trustworthy information as to what is wrong in current practice, and as to the sort of typical acts and refusals to act in which genuine Christianity would show itself. Such consultation on an extensive and systematic scale is a necessary preliminary to any adequate Christian casuistry, and to the organization of a legitimate Christian moral opinion.

Thirdly, we clearly need careful re-statement for Christians of the responsibility of wealth. Strong and solemn are St. Paul's words. 'Having food and raiment, let us be therewith content. But they that will be rich fall into temptation and a snare, and into many foolish and hurtful lusts, which drown men in destruction and perdition. For the love of money is a root of all evil; which while some coveted after, they have erred from the faith, and pierced themselves through with many sorrows[1].' One of the most distinguished of living men I once heard say that luxury was like the strings with which the Liliputians tied Gulliver; each thread was weak in itself so that any one could break it, but together they held him fast more tightly than strong cords. So with the little things of luxury; they grow upon people, the things we say we 'cannot do without.' In their accumulation they tie society down, and make us the slaves of innumerable wants not really requisite for life, or health, or happiness. We want to re-state the obligation of Christian simplicity. We want to press upon Christians the conviction that wealth is not a justification of selfish luxury, but a solemn trust for the good of mankind. Beyond all question, whatever may be the func-

[1] 1 Tim. vi. 8-10.

tion of the State in regard to wealth, it is the function of the Christian Church to emphasize the responsibility which it involves upon the consciences of its members more, very much more, than has been done in the past.

Lastly, in regard to the position of women in view of the modern movement for what is called her emancipation. Obviously this is a matter on which the Christian Church is bound to have clear teaching, and to make it heard. I believe that no society or system could put women so high as Christianity puts them, or could give so great a dignity to womanhood as Christianity gives it. But Christianity dignifies womanhood not by ignoring or confusing the differences, physiological and moral, which obtain between men and women; but by assigning them distinct spheres, in view of the distinctive characteristics, which all experience at least justifies us in attaching to the sexes.

What is the position of women in Holy Scripture? There is the position of the wife, that position at the head of the household which is held up to our admiration in the memorable panegyric upon the mistress of the household in the last chapter of the Book of Proverbs. Is there any position in life more dignified? Is there any priesthood higher than the ministry of the mother of the family? And then there is that ministry of mercy, belonging in a measure specially to unmarried women and widows. These, St. Paul says, are in a special sense free to consecrate themselves to the service of Christ and His poor. This is the second position for women that Holy Scripture recognizes. It was the shame of our society fifty years ago that it had so largely taken away the dignity of unmarried life or failed to recognize it. Besides the normal positions of women, we must also recognize exceptional cases :—there are in the New Testament prophetesses, like Philip's daughters. This position, I suppose, corresponds more or less to what we see in the case of a St. Catherine or a St. Theresa, if not to the extraordinary mission of a Joan of Arc. These are clearly exceptional cases. The position of a public preacher, or active politician, the Church would not, I suppose, normally recognize as appropriate to women. The inclination to such positions she would, I think, with the authority of the New Testament behind her, keep under severe restraint, and would only allow of such missions when there was an over-mastering sense of divine vocation.

I do not want to go into details. My object has been rather to quicken our consciousness of the moral mission of the Church. But I have endeavoured to specify four departments in which we need to think out and re-state what is the Christian moral law. The Church ought to be giving clearer teaching than in fact she is giving in regard to the law of marriage, in regard to commercial morality, in regard to the responsibility of wealth, in regard to the position and true dignity of women.

In the past sixty years there has been a great advance among us along what one may call the lines of personal sanctification, and also in developing special forms of religious self-dedication. Wonderful, surely, has been the development of the nursing profession, and of sisterhoods, the revival of spiritual discipline, of the ideal of the priesthood and of the evangelical freedom of the celibate life. All this that God has done among us gives us the greatest cause for encouragement. What now seems to be needed, is that we should pay special attention to the sanctification of common social life[1], laying down in clear terms the moral law of Christianity and pressing its fuller observance upon the conscience of Churchmen. Thus the world will understand that, as the Church has a distinct creed and a distinct worship, so she has also a distinctive moral law for social life, which is to be her characteristic mark in all sorts of societies and under all sorts of conditions.

V.

This moral law, unchanging as it is, we are to seek to commend to the consciences of all men, specially by finding its affinity to the moral tendencies and aspirations of our own time. We are to discern the signs of the

[1] See in the *Dublin Review*, July, 1892, an article by Dr. Barry on the life of Fr. Hecker, pp. 80-2.

times, for good as for evil: always to keep our eye on the unchanging law of Christ, and also always on the changing wants and aspirations of men round about us; so shall we fill the office of interpreters translating the ancient precepts into current language, bringing forth out of our treasures, like wise stewards, things new and old, commending our message to every man's conscience in the sight of God.

Why do we not discern the signs of the times? If we look abroad and ask what is the meaning of the current body of right social aspiration in the world to-day, you find it such as is not infrequently expressed in the word socialism. Now socialism is generally taken to imply a certain policy in regard to the functions of the State, with which we need not now concern ourselves. In the New Testament the function assigned to the State, is that of administering the divine law of justice among men, and for the realization of this function among ourselves a good deal still remains for political reforms to accomplish. Whether the Christian law, so far as it may be said to go beyond the law of justice, can ever become the law of the State is another question. But socialism expresses not only a state policy but also a moral ideal. As a moral ideal it is profoundly Christian, and I believe that the great Christian principle of the brotherhood of man as based upon the fatherhood of God sums up all that is best in the social and moral aspiration of our time, whether it does or does not call itself Christian. In past ages we have allowed Calvinism to rob the imagination of Christians of that rich treasure, that masterthought, of the fatherhood of God—His impartial, individual, disciplinary love for all men whom He has created: also we have allowed the love of luxury and power in privileged classes to rob us of the corresponding truth of the brotherhood of men—the capacity of all men for brotherhood and the realization of that capacity in the 'brotherhood' of the Church. The time has come to restore to men's minds and hearts the full vivid power of these central conceptions.

It is a department of this work of restoration,

to bring back into general recognition the originally representative and fraternal character of the institutions of the Church. Thus the Christian ministry, the Christian episcopate, runs back behind the association with which it has become encrusted in days of English aristocracy and mediaeval feudalism. It runs back to what one may call the constitutional fraternity of the early Church. In the Church of the Empire the episcopate, and indeed the presbyterate also, had a representative character. Real representative government may be said to have had its origin in the Christian ministry. These Church officers were indeed ordained from above, in accordance with the principle of apostolic succession; but they were elected in correspondence with the representative principle. And patristic writers emphasized this representative character of Church officers sometimes, it seems, almost as much as the necessity of due and proper ordination and succession[1]. These are principles to which we cannot return hurriedly, and their application at this particular

[1] See *The Church and the Ministry*, pp. 97-107.

moment is complicated by a dominant fallacy—the identification of the Christian layman with the English citizen. Now it is in every organization of men a fundamental principle that social rights only correspond to social duties done. Where people are not living by their Church principles, and doing their duty as Churchmen, they lose the rights and privileges of Churchmen. But when this misunderstanding has been cleared away, and the layman is recognized to be one fulfilling his Church obligations, the principle of representation ought to be applied. We do, then, need to watch and pray and labour for the recovery of that more truly representative character which did belong to Church institutions in early times.

I have come to the end of that small portion of a great task which it has been possible even to attempt to accomplish in four lectures. I have been speaking of the nature of the Church's mission and of some of the tasks which lie before her. Before we separate let me say a word of the power in which we go forth to our duty.

VI.

We believe that Christ, on whom our faith and hope and love are fixed, is the master of all ages and of all men. It is true of every great man that he passes in a measure beyond the conditions of a particular age, and gains a certain universality; it is true in a unique sense of Christ. He was very God. He took our manhood into His divine personality. The result is a character which is truly human, but which has none of the limitations which narrow human nature. He took those limitations which belong necessarily to humanity—the limitations which make possible the exercise of a really human faith and virtue—not the limitations which characterize an Englishman, or a Chinaman, or a particular age, or sex, or class. Jesus Christ is the catholic man; His appeal is to all men of all ages. His example is universal; His teaching is applicable to all time; and the grace which makes it possible for us really to correspond to His appeal, to follow His example, to accept His teaching, is nothing short of the communication to us of His own unchanging self, His own eternal and His human spirit. It is the inward presence of Jesus Christ, the inward relation in which we stand to Him, that makes His example always, for the sons of faith, practical and realizable. For Jesus who is 'passed into the heavens,' ' made higher than the heavens,' is yet by the Spirit brought nearer to us than ever He was to the Apostles on earth ; the Spirit links the humanity of every member of the Lord's body to Him as He sits in glorified manhood at the right hand of God. The Spirit's presence is the presence of Jesus, as the presence of Jesus is the presence of the Father, for the holy persons of the Trinity are in inseparable unity. Thus the Christ, God in manhood, is present in the Christian, in as true a sense of the word 'presence' as that word can bear, by spiritual force and reality. Christ in us is the hope of glory. And He, whose example we have before our eyes in the pages of the Gospels is working inwardly in our hearts, to purify us gradually and mould us into His own incomparable likeness. This

The Mission of the Church in Society.

which is the source of our own encouragement gives us also our hope for men. It is the great privilege of the Christian to look behind all discouragements on the surface of humanity, to fasten upon its hidden capacity for God, and to hope for every man who does not obstinately and persistently refuse the divine offer. They are few, we may hope, who thus finally refuse God. We are willing rather to think of men as weak and wandering, and to have hope for them. We have ground of hope because we know what the love of God for each soul means, what is the infinite self-sacrifice of the Son of God. And if there is any turning towards God in the heart of a man, though it be tentative and inchoate, we believe that there is eternity, there is the world beyond the grave, for the purpose of God to take full effect.

We shall lose heart and courage in our ministry except so far as our mind is constantly fixed upon Christ; both as giving us our moral ideal for men and as supplying the forces of recovery. With our eyes fixed upon Christ, and upon eternity, we have justification for believing beyond belief, and hoping beyond hope for the souls of men; and, in fact, our power of recovering men depends on our power of hoping for them and believing in them. If you have ceased to believe in any human soul you have, by that very fact, lost all chance of helping it towards recovery. Your power of recovering men depends on your power of believing in them; and your power of believing in them depends on the constancy with which you contemplate the mind of Christ towards them and the eternal destiny which lies before them. It is not our wealth, or position, or the historical dignity of our Church which will save men. It is simply the power of Christ. And, in fact, the real spiritual power of the Church has not risen and fallen with its secular position. There is a famous answer attributed, I believe, to St. Thomas Aquinas when, on the occasion of some Papal Jubilee, the bags of gold were being carried past into the treasury of Peter, and the Pope said to him—' Peter could not say now, "Silver and gold have I none"':

The Mission of the Church in Society. 149

'No, your Blessedness,' replied Thomas, 'Nor can he say, "In the name of Jesus Christ of Nazareth rise up and walk."'

It is in the strength of Jesus then truly and literally that we are to go out comforting others with the comfort wherewith we ourselves are comforted of God[1].

And, oh! do not narrow that word 'comfort.' We are to minister to the broken-hearted, the sick, the weary, the dying; we are to comfort them in the ordinary sense of comfort, with absolution, and solace, and peace. But we have not only to do with the broken, the feeble, the exhausted, but also with the young, the high-spirited, the enthusiastic and energetic. The mission of the Church applies just as much to these as to those. It is as much our privilege and our duty to put courage and confidence, and a sense of service and hope, into the hearts of the enthusiastic and promising, as it is to console penitents, and to bind up the broken-hearted. 'As a young man marrieth a virgin, so shall thy sons

[1] See app. note 17.

marry thee.' We must be inspired by the spirit and meaning of the Church, so that we can present her to men as something that can enlist their hopes and energies, and vitalize all their highest faculties. 'They that seek the Lord shall renew their strength; they shall mount up with wings as eagles; they shall run, and not be weary; they shall walk, and not faint.' We have a great work before us; a work for the doing of which divine encouragements are given; but it is a work that needs all the best energies that humanity has to offer.

APPENDED NOTES.

Note 1, to p. 18.

The witness to the doctrine of the visible Church in Clement and Ignatius. 'Clement,' says Prof. Pfleiderer truly (*Hibbert Lectures*, p. 252), 'most characteristically connected the new law of the Church with the two models of the political and military organization of the Roman state and the sacerdotal hierarchy of the Jewish theocracy' (i.e. it was to his mind an organized, and divinely organized, body): but the Professor is not justified in regarding this as in opposition to St. Paul's teaching of justification. See above pp. 68 ff. and *The Church and the Ministry* (Longmans), pp. 49 f., also on Clement, pp. 309 f. 316 f.

The witness of Clement is very explicit to the Church in its general idea. The witness of Ignatius is much more emphatic to the threefold ministry of bishops, priests, and deacons. This he regards (1) as essential to the existence of a Church, (2) as based on the ordinances of the Apostles, (3) as coextensive with the Church. See *Ch. and Min.*, p. 300 f. This testimony is quite compatible with that afforded by the Didache and by Clement if it be recognized that the superior apostolic, prophetic, or (in the later sense) episcopal order was in some districts not localized in particular Churches till a subsequent date: see above pp. 29, 30, and *Ch. and Min.*, pp. 333 ff.

NOTE 2, to p. 22.

Archdeacon Sinclair, in his recent charge, *The Church, Invisible, Visible, Catholic, National* (Eliot Stock, 1892), appears to put the individual relation of the soul to God first, to regard it as logically prior to, and independent of, church-membership, and to make the association of Christians into societies a subsequent act. See p. 2. 'But just as believers having this personal relation to their Lord would be in a spiritual sense as the branches to the vine, as the limbs to the head, so they would naturally form, under the Divine guidance, a society among themselves in their relation to each other on earth.' May I call attention on this subject to some words of the present bishop of London in a noble sermon entitled 'Individualism and Catholicism.' See *Twelve Sermons preached at the consecration of Truro Cathedral* (Wells, Gardner & Masters, 1888), pp. 17-20.

Appended Notes. 153

'We are sometimes asked to think that the Church only exists in the union of believers, and has no reality of its own. Now, it is perfectly clear that in the New Testament the idea of the Church is not that. Men talk sometimes as if a church could be constituted simply by Christians coming together and uniting themselves into one body for the purpose. Men speak as if Christians came first, and the Church after; as if the origin of the Church was in the wills of individual Christians who composed it. But, on the contrary, throughout the teaching of the Apostles we see that it is the Church that comes first and the members of it afterwards. Men were not brought to Christ and then determined that they would live in a community. Men were not brought to Christ to believe in Him and his Cross, and to recognize the duty of worshipping the Heavenly Father in His name, and then decided that it would be a great help to their religion that they should join one another in that worship, and should be united in the bonds of fellowship for that purpose. In the New Testament, on the contrary, the Kingdom of Heaven is already in existence, and men are invited into it. The Church takes its origin, not in the will of man, but in the will of the Lord Jesus Christ. He sent forth His Apostles; the Apostles received their commission from Him; they were not organs of the congregation; they were ministers of the Lord Himself. He sent them forth to gather all the thousands that they could reach within His fold; but they came first, and the members came afterwards; and the Church in all its dignity and glory was quite independent of the members that were brought within it. Everywhere men are called in; they do not come in, and make the Church by coming. They are called in to that which already exists; they are recognized as members when they are within; but their membership depends upon their admission, and not upon their constituting themselves into a body in the sight of the Lord. . . . .

'This individualism of which I speak has too much truth in it to fail in strength. It cannot be counter-balanced by anything but insisting on what the Church of the New Testament really is; making men everywhere understand that the Church is a body which lives from age to age: adapting itself to all times and all circumstances: finding spiritual life for all characters; supplying the means of grace for every variety in humanity. It is for this that we insist upon the succession of the ministry, because we find the Church from the very beginning flowing out of the ministry. He distorts that conception of the ministry who ever allows it to be the means of separating clergy from laity, and making men think that the great body consists of the clergy only, or that the clergy only are the life of the body. The purpose of that succession is to link the Church of the present from generation to generation, back, by steps that cannot be mistaken, to the first appointment of the Apostles by the Lord. The purpose of that succession is to make men feel the unity of the body as it comes down the stream of history, and, if possible, to touch their hearts with some sense of that power which the Lord bequeathed when He ascended up on high and gave gifts to men; with some sense of that grace which He promised when He said that He would be with us always, even to the end of the world; some sense of that undying life which shall still, until He comes again, unite those who love Him with Himself, and spread the knowledge of His name throughout the human race. To this persistence of the Church as a living body a Cathedral ever bears a silent but visible witness; the seat of Bishop after Bishop, not ruling in his own name; not by virtue of his own abilities; not giving to posterity the narrow legacy of his own opinions nor institutions that shall for ever represent himself, but each in succession handing on the life and power of the Church of Christ.'

Archdeacon Sinclair makes much of the 'invisible' and 'ideal' Church, of which we are constituted members by faith. No doubt this idea took powerful hold of the minds of the Reformers and of later Protestants; yet as the Lutheran Rothe pointed out (see *Ch. and Min.*, p. 19) it does not represent the thought of the early Church, nor does it that of the New Testament. It is true (1) that part of the Church, i. e. that in Paradise, is invisible to us: and (2) that many conscientious good men are not members of the Church now, who yet will, we trust, become members of the Church in Paradise. Also (3) that all baptized persons are as such members of the one Church on earth, even though they are living in very broken relation to it. Also (4) that the Church does not represent the whole sphere of the divine action, and is not therefore simply identical with the kingdom of God. But the Church so far as it is on earth, means nothing else than the visible organized body of baptized persons, worthy or unworthy. The word 'Church' throughout the New Testament stands for the same thing, and not at one time for a visible society, at another for an ideal or invisible relation.

NOTE 3, to p. 24.

Necessity of sacraments not absolute. See St. Thom. Aq. P. iii. Q. 68. Art. 2. 'Deus .... cuius potentia sacramentis visibilibus non alligatur, cf. S. Aug. *Quaestt. in Levit.* 84. Proinde colligitur invisibilem sanctificationem quibusdam affuisse et profuisse sine visibilibus sacramentis .. nec tamen ideo sacramentum visibile contemnendum est: nam contemptor eius invisibiliter sanctificari nullo modo potest.' See also Andrewes in *Libr. of Angl. Cath. Theol.*, Sermons vol. v. p. 92 'Gratia Dei non alligatur mediis.'

NOTE 4, TO p. 28.

Irenaeus on the elements of the Christian religion.
The language of Irenaeus, the great representative in the second century of the principle of apostolic tradition, is very striking. *C. Haer*, iy. 33, 8. 'The true knowledge (the Christian religion) is the doctrine of the Apostles and the ancient system of the Church in all the world; and the character of the body of Christ according to the successions of the bishops to whom they (the Apostles) delivered the Church in each separate place; the complete use moreover of the Scripture which has come down to our time, preserved without corruption, receiving neither addition nor loss; its public reading without falsification; legitimate and careful exposition according to the scriptures, without peril and without blasphemy; and the pre-eminent gift of love.'

NOTE 5, to p. 43.

The contents of the New Testament 'tradition.'
We should gather from the New Testament that the original 'catechetical teaching' contained (*a*) instruction in the facts of our Lord's life, death, resurrection, &c., cf. Luke i. 1-4; 1 Cor. xi. 23, xv. 3-4. (*b*) instruction in the meaning of sacred rites, baptism, laying on of hands, eucharist, Heb. vi. 1-6; cf. Rom. vi. 3; 1 Cor x. 15-16, xi. 23 ff.; cf. Acts ii. 38. This would have included the learning of

the Lord's Prayer, see *Didache*, 8. (*c*) Instruction in the moral obligations of 'the way' and in the 'last things' Heb. vi. 1-2; 1 Thess. iv. 1-2, v. 2. We must add to this, what I think almost all New Testament writings would imply, (*d*) instruction in the meaning of 'the Name'—the Name of the Father, the Son, and the Holy Ghost. (The Judaic, semi-Christian, character of the instruction in the *Didache*, whether moral, doctrinal, or sacramental, see the *Ch. and the Min.*, pp. 411 f., makes its emphatic witness to the Threefold Name (see c. 7) the more important). In all cases the references I have given above are not references to the teaching of the New Testament books, but the teaching which those books imply to have been already given.

NOTE 6, to p. 51.

The Anglican doctrine of the sacraments. Nothing surely can be richer or better than Hooker's teaching on the sacraments in principle. *E. P.* v. 50, 56 ff. If all parties could agree on what he teaches *positively*, it would be well for the Church of England. And it is not to be forgotten how strongly, and surely rightly, Hooker, with the older Catholic writers, insists, against some more recent schoolmen, that God is the direct agent in the bestowal of grace on the occasion of each sacrament—'solum Deum producere gratiam ad praesentiam sacramentorum.' *E. P.* vi. 6 10-11.

NOTE 7, to p. 52.

The Anglican requirement of the apostolic succession. On this subject let me refer to the careful language of Prof. Stanton, *The Place of Authority in Religious Belief* (Longmans, 1891), pp. 204 ff., and 225 ff. See also the *Catena* of Anglican Divines in *Tracts for the Times*, No. 74. One may recognize that as a fact the Anglican divines of the seventeenth century admitted exceptions to the necessity of episcopal ordination without either thinking their teaching on this head seriously dangerous, or on the other hand regarding it as quite adequate to ancient standards. Archdeacon Sinclair does not, to my mind (l. c. pp. 55 ff.), use these Anglican divines quite fairly. To mention two points: they are speaking of Protestants who 'want an ordinary succession *without their own fault*, out of invincible ignorance or necessity,' or 'where bishops could not be had.' Now these qualifications greatly limit the application of their words. Secondly, they show no tenderness at all to schismatics in their own country. If I were a Nonconformist I would sooner be dealt with by a modern High Churchman than by a Caroline divine, though the modern High Churchman taught by experience has returned to the simpler ancient doctrine of the apostolic succession as necessary not indeed to the salvation of an individual, but to the constitution of a Church.

Note 8, to p. 56.

The meaning of the word 'spiritual.' Cf. Milligan, *Resurrection of our Lord* (Macmillan, 1st ed.) note 15, p. 247 : 'An element of confusion is introduced into all our thoughts upon this subject by the ambiguity of such words as "spirit" and "spiritual." We are apt to think of them as antithetical to "body" and "bodily." How far this is from the view of the New Testament the single passage 1 Cor. xv. 44 is sufficient to prove. The antithesis of scripture is not of the spiritual and the bodily, but that of the spiritual and the carnal.'

This passage is perhaps too strongly expressed. Thus 'spirit' as applied to God, carries with it (e.g. St. John iv. 24) associations of immateriality; again, the 'spirit' of man is opposed to his 'body' 1 Cor. v. 3, 1 Thess. v. 23. But the glorified Christ in His risen body is also called simply 'spirit' 1 Cor. xv. 45, and the adjective 'spiritual' (1 Cor. x. 3, xv. 44) or the phrase 'according to the spirit' (Gal. iv. 29) carries with it no sort of opposition to materiality: that is spiritual which is according to the law of the spirit, or the expression of spirit.

Note 9, to p. 63.

Gnostic esotericism and Christian universality. On this subject see Lightfoot's note on Col. i. 28; and Neander's *Ch. Hist.* (Bohn's trans.), ii. pp. 33-34.

The effect of the Gnostic controversy on the sacramental and ecclesiastical teaching of Christianity appears most clearly in Ignatius' letters, Irenaeus B. iii. 1-4, iv. 17-18, v. 2-3. Tertullian, *De Res. Carn.* 8 and *De Praescr.*

NOTE 10, to p. 65.

Tertullian on the simplicity of Christian sacraments. See *De Bapt.* 2. ' Nihil adeo est, quod tam obduret mentes hominum, quam simplicitas divinorum operum quae in actu videtur et magnificentia quae in effectu repromittitur : ut hic quoque quoniam tanta simplicitate sine pompa, sine apparatu novo aliquo, denique sine sumptu homo in aqua demissus et inter pauca verba tinctus non multo vel nihilo mundior resurgit, eo incredibilis existimetur consecutio aeternitatis. Mentior, si non e contrario idolorum sollemnia vel arcana de suggestu et apparatu deque sumptu fidem et auctoritatem sibi exstruunt. Pro misera incredulitas, quae denegas Deo proprietates suas, simplicitatem et potestatem.'

NOTE 11, to p. 68.

Goethe on the sacramental system. There is a very remarkable passage in Goethe's Autobiography (*Dichtung und Wahrheit*, see Bohn's Trans., vol. i. p. 245-248), where, complaining of the paucity of Protestant sacraments, he writes: 'In moral and religious, as well as in physical and civil matters, a man does not like to do anything on the spur of the moment; he needs a sequence such as results in habit; what he is to love and perform, he cannot represent to himself as single or isolated, and if he is to repeat anything willingly, it must not have become strange to him. As the Protestant worship lacks fulness in general, so, if it be investigated in detail, it will be found that the Protestant has too few sacraments, nay, indeed, he has only one in which he is himself an actor—the Lord's Supper: for baptism he sees only when it is performed on others, and is not greatly edified by it. The sacraments are the highest part of religion, the symbols to our senses of an extraordinary divine favour and grace. In the Lord's Supper earthly lips are to receive a divine Being embodied, and partake of an heavenly under the form of an earthly nourishment. This idea is just the same in all Christian churches; whether the sacrament is taken with more or less submission to the mystery, with more or less accommodation to what is intelligible; it always remains a great and holy action, which in reality takes the place of the possible or impossible, the place of that which man can neither attain nor do without. But such a sacrament should not stand alone; no Christian can partake of it with the true joy for which it is given, if the symbolical or sacramental sense is not fostered within him. He must be accustomed to regard the inner religion of the heart and that of the external church as perfectly

Appended Notes.

one; as the great universal sacrament, which again divides itself into so many others, and communicates to these parts its holiness, indestructibleness, and eternity.'

This is followed by a wonderfully appreciative account of the sequence of sacraments, adapted to all stages of human life, in the Catholic Church.

NOTE 12, to p. 71.

Christians have no need to ask for the Spirit. See Moule, *Veni Creator* (Hodder & Stoughton, 1890), pp. 222-3. The Christian Church has in fact habitually invoked the Holy Spirit—'Veni, Creator Spiritus' 'Veni, sancte Spiritus'—and such language has a clear meaning in view of the fact that what God has given He is still perpetually giving. But the fact about the New Testament language is as stated in the text. See Rom. viii. 9, 15, 16; Gal. v. 25; Eph. iv. 30; 1 Thess. v. 19; Heb. vi. 4; 1 John iii. 24; cf. 1 Tim. iv. 14; 2 Tim. i. 6.

NOTE 13, to p. 73.

Infants who are proper subjects of baptism. It is the general teaching of the Church that the children of non-Christian parents, are not, till they come to years of discretion, fit subjects of baptism, unless their parents give them to the Church. See St. Thom. Aq. *Summa Theol.* P. iii. Q. 68. Art. 10.

(This decision he bases on the fact that they have not yet in themselves the exercise of will; that it is against the will, and so against the natural right of the parent: that it generates scandal through relapses.) On the other hand, the Church since St. Paul, regards the children of a Christian parent, as fit subjects for baptism. See 1 Cor. vii. 14. The children are 'holy,' i. e., as Tertullian interprets, 'designati sanctitati ac per hoc etiam saluti' (*De An.* 29). The reason is that the faith of the parent offers the child for baptism, and truly represents it. Thus the 68th canon (of 1603) decrees the penalty of suspension for three months upon any minister who refuses to christen according to the form of the Book of Common Prayer any child that is brought to him upon Sundays or Holydays to be christened. Besides the faith of the parents a guarantee is also provided in the faith of the sponsors who represent the Church. 'Children,' says St. Augustine, 'are presented to receive spiritual grace not so much by those who bear them in their arms—though by them too if they are also good Christians—as by the whole society of the faithful' (*Ep.* 98. 5).

The principle in all this is that *faith is to be required when baptism is to be administered*; either the faith of the person to be baptized or, in the case of a child, of those who undertake for him, his parents or the Church. This representative faith, which guarantees the Christian education of children, is plainly demanded by our baptismal office, as a condition of baptism. We violate then a fundamental principle, and degrade a sacrament to the level of a charm, if we get children to be baptized indiscriminately, i. e. without reference to their Christian bringing up. It must be wrong to put undue pressure upon parents to have their children baptized where it is even reasonably certain that they will not either act towards them, *or allow the Church to act*, as Christian parents should. Some initiative on the part of the parents, or some guarantee on behalf of the Church, ought to be asked for : see, on the general subject, Maskell, *Holy Baptism* (Pickering, 1848), pp. 336–348.

NOTE 14, to p. 93.

Science cannot proceed without assumptions. See Herbert Spencer, *First Principles* (Williams & Norgate, 5th ed. 1887), pp. 137 f. ' In what way, then, must philosophy set out ? The developed intelligence is framed upon certain organized and consolidated conceptions of which it cannot divest itself: and which it can no more stir without using than the body can stir without help of its limbs. In what way, then, is it possible for intelligence, striving after Philosophy, to give any account of these conceptions, and to show either their validity or their invalidity ? There is but one way : those of them which are vital, or cannot be severed from the rest without vital dissolution, must be assumed as true *provisionally*. The fundamental intuitions that are necessary to the process of thinking, must be temporarily accepted as unquestionable : leaving the assumption of their unquestionableness to be justified by the results. How is it to be justified by the results ? As any other assumption is justified— by ascertaining that all the conclusions deducible from it, correspond with the facts as directly observed —by showing the agreement between the experiences it leads us to anticipate and the actual experiences. *There is no method of establishing the validity of any belief, except that of showing its entire congruity with all other beliefs.'*

I have italicized the last sentence, and would compare with it an admirable passage on the relation of philosophy to ordinary assumptions, scientific and religious, in E. Caird's *Philosophy of Kant* (Maclehose, Glasgow, 1877) pp. 34-5. The line of thought may be pursued in Holland's *Logic and Life* (Longmans) Sermons i-iii, and in Newman's *Univ. Sermons*, 'Implicit and Explicit Reason.'

NOTE 15, to p. 100.

Evolution and its relation to Religious Thought. See an excellent work, with this title, by the distinguished American man of science, Prof. Leconte (Chapman & Hall). The first two parts of the

Appended Notes. 167

book are occupied with the statement of the theory of evolution and of the evidence on which it rests. The third part considers the relation of the theory to Theism in general and Christianity in particular. (From the theological point of view Prof. Leconte's remarks upon the theory of moral evil are surely inadequate, ed. 2. pp. 369 ff.)

NOTE 16, to p. 134.

The resolutions of the Conference of Bishops of the Anglican Communion (July 1888) *in regard to Divorce.* See *Encyclical Letter with Resolutions and Reports* (S. P. C. K. 1888) Resol. 4.

'(1) That inasmuch as our Lord's words expressly forbid divorce, except in the case of fornication or adultery, the Christian Church cannot recognize divorce in any other than the excepted case, or give any sanction to the marriage of any person who has been divorced contrary to this law, during the life of the other party.

'(2) That under no circumstances ought the guilty party in the case of a divorce for adultery, to be regarded, during the life-time of the innocent party, as a fit recipient of the blessing of the Church on marriage.

'(3) That recognizing that there always has been a difference of opinion in the Church on the question whether our Lord meant to forbid marriage to the innocent party in a divorce for adultery, the conference recommends that the clergy should not be instructed to refuse the sacraments or other privileges of the Church to those who, under civil sanctions, are thus married.

'(4) That whereas doubt has been entertained whether our Lord meant to permit such marriage to the innocent party, the Conference are unwilling to suggest any precise instruction in the matter.' The Bishop of the diocese is to decide 'whether clergy would be justified in refraining from pronouncing the blessing of the Church on such unions.'

These Pan-Anglican Conferences are not legitimate synods, provincial or general, and the language of this resolution implies the recognition of this fact. But the resolutions represent fairly the present mind of Anglican bishops, given with a due sense of spiritual responsibility. For 'the difference of opinion which there has always been in the Church' on the respect of the re-marriage of the innocent party, reference may be made to the *Library of the Fathers*. Tertullian, Note O. pp. 431 f.

It is interesting to note that Dr. Liddon, in a letter to the *Guardian* of Sept. 19, 1888, recording Dr. Döllinger's general satisfaction at the results of the Pan-Anglican Conference writes: 'To advert to a point which has caused some anxiety—the Conference was, as he believed, right in recommending that the clergy should not be instructed to refuse the sacraments to the innocent party who remarried after a divorce for adultery. He still had no doubt that πορνεία in St. Matt. v. 32 and xix. 9 could not mean μοιχεία but must refer to something that had taken place before the marriage contract. The decision of the Conference was, however, justified by the history of opinion in the Church, about which he had more to say than could be compressed into a letter.'

But the Anglican 107th Canon of 1603, with the Western Church as a whole, takes the stricter line of forbidding the re-marriage of either party in a divorce and separation ' a thoro et mensa ' during each other's life. This line is undoubtedly more logical, but there does not seem to be adequate authority for *enforcing* it.

NOTE 17, to p. 149.

Christ our example and our inward life. The Roman Collect for the Octave of the Epiphany expresses this thought very beautifully:—' Deus cuius unigenitus in substantia nostrae carnis apparuit, praesta, quaesumus, ut per eum, quem similem nobis foris agnovimus, intus reformari mereamur: qui tecum vivit.'

CANON GORE'S WORKS.

Crown 8vo, 3s. 6d.

AN EXPOSITION OF THE EPISTLE TO THE EPHESIANS. By the Rev. CHARLES GORE, Canon of Westminster.

'A new work by Canon Gore is an ecclesiastical event The book is a popular exposition in the best sense, conveying to the simplest understanding the results of the best modern knowledge of this epistle. The general effect of the book is bracing. . . . . Surely no one can read this book without a quickened desire to be a Christian.'—*Guardian.*

'It is a brave and earnest book straight from the heart of an earnest and brave man.'—*Independent.*

Crown 8vo, 3s. 6d. Ninth Thousand.

THE SERMON ON THE MOUNT. A Practical Explanation. By the Rev. CHARLES GORE, Canon of Westminster.

CONTENTS: The Sermon; The Beatitudes in General; The Beatitudes in Detail; The Deepening of the Law; The Christian Motive; The Lord's Prayer; Unworldliness; Christian Characteristics; Concluding Warnings.

Crown 8vo, 6s. Twenty-first Thousand.

LUX MUNDI. A Cheaper Edition. A Series of Studies in the Religion of the Incarnation. By Various Writers. Edited by the Rev. CHARLES GORE, D.D.

Crown 8vo, 2s. 6d. Sixth Thousand.

THE MISSION OF THE CHURCH. Four Lectures delivered in the Cathedral Church of St. Asaph. By the Rev. CHARLES GORE, late Principal of Pusey House, Oxford, Editor of 'Lux Mundi.'

CONTENTS:—I. The Mission of the Church; II. Unity within the Church of England; III. The Relation of the Church to Independent and Hostile Opinion; IV. The Mission of the Church in Society; Appended Notes.

'It is a twofold work—to sanctify what can be hallowed, to pass judgment on that which must be condemned. From this point of view the interest of Mr. Gore's new book is great.'—*Church Quarterly.*

8vo, 7s. 6d. Tenth Thousand.

THE BAMPTON LECTURES, 1891; THE INCARNATION OF THE SON OF GOD. By the Rev. CHARLES GORE, D.D., late Principal of Pusey House, Oxford, Editor of 'Lux Mundi.'

8vo, 7s. 6d. Third Thousand.

DISSERTATIONS ON SUBJECTS CONNECTED WITH THE INCARNATION. By the Rev. CHARLES GORE, Canon of Westminster.

8vo, 10s. 6d.

ESSAYS ON CHURCH REFORM. Edited the by Rev. CHARLES GORE, M.A., Honorary Chaplain to the Queen.

Crown 8vo, 3s. 6d.

AN EXPOSITION OF THE EPISTLE TO THE ROMANS. By the Rev. CHARLES GORE, D.D. Uniform with the 'Epistle of the Ephesians.' [*To appear before Lent,* 1899.

JOHN MURRAY, Albemarle Street.

SELECTION OF
MR. MURRAY'S RELIGIOUS WORKS.

Crown 8vo, 6d.

THE LORD'S PRAYER. By the late EDWARD MEYRICK GOULBURN, D.D., sometime Dean of Norwich, Author of 'Thoughts on Personal Religion,' &c.

'The work is so full, so rich in thought and learning, so calm and earnest at the same time. One revels in such a volume. It is entirely representative of the culture and piety of a typical Anglican divine. We have known nothing better on that most wonderful and beautiful prayer.'—*Literary World.*

Crown 8vo, 3s. 6d.

SERMONS TO YOUNG BOYS. Delivered at Elstree School, by the Rev. F. de W. LUSHINGTON.

'Amid many sermons to boys these stand somewhat alone both for their simplicity and also because they are addressed to younger boys than are school sermons of the common type.'—*Guardian.*

Crown 8vo, 7s. 6d.

THE LIFE AND LETTERS OF THE REV. JOHN BACCHUS DYKES, M.A., &c. With Portrait.

'Will not only be read with interest by the multitude of those who have loved his many hymn tunes, which have become almost inseparable from certain popular hymns, but as a study of an earnest and devout Churchman it has a very considerable value.'—*Times.*

'To say that millions every Sunday sing the tunes of J. B. Dykes is to be beside the mark.'—*Birmingham Gazette.*

Demy 8vo, 14s.

MINISTERIAL PRIESTHOOD: Six Chapters Preliminary to the Study of the Ordinal. With an Inquiry into the Truth of Christian Priesthood, and an Appendix on the recent Roman Controversy. By R. C. MOBERLY, D.D.

'As one of the authors of 'Lux Mundi,' Canon Moberly's exposition is distinguished by the high qualities which have made the school to which the writer belongs so influential in the Church of England.'—*Manchester Guardian.*

Second Edition, royal 16mo, 3s. 6d.

LATER GLEANINGS: Theological and Ecclesiastical. By the Right Hon. W. E. GLADSTONE.

CONTENTS:—The Dawn of Creation and Worship; Proem to Genesis; Robert Elsmere: The Battle of Belief; Ingersoll on Christianity; The Elizabethan Settlement; Queen Elizabeth and the Church of England; The Church under Henry; Professor Huxley and the Swine Miracle; The Places of Heresy and Schism; True and False Conceptions of the Atonement; The Lord's Day; Ancient Beliefs in a Future State; Soliloquium and Postscription the Pope and Anglican Orders.

Crown 8vo, 5s.

THE CHILDHOOD AND YOUTH OF OUR LORD: Based on the Gospel Narrative, and the Manners and Customs of the Jews of Palestine. By the Rev. J. BROUGH, M.A., Chaplain to the Forces.

'This work shows careful study and an intimate knowledge of the Bible and Biblical expositions. We can strongly recommend it, and honestly thank the author for his book.'—*Manchester Guardian.*

JOHN MURRAY, Albemarle Street.

www.ingramcontent.com/pod-product-compliance
Lightning Source LLC
Chambersburg PA
CBHW020242170426
43202CB00008B/191